GEORGE DIEPSTRA & GREGORY J. LAUGHERY

FROM
EVOLUTION
TO
EDEN

MAKING SENSE OF EARLY GENESIS

D1566679

destinēe

Published by Destinée S.A., www.destinee.ch

Cover and interior by Per-Ole Lind.
Cover art: "The Garden of Earthly Delights" by
   Hieronymus Bosch, dated between 1490 and 1510.
Set with Garamond (1530) and Akzidenz (1896).

ISBN: 978-1-938367-19-9

destinēe

CONTENTS

ACKNOWLEDGEMENTS

We are deeply grateful to Susanna Young, Gabrielle Young, and Per-Ole Lind for their excellent contributions to this book. There are many others to thank, but it would be difficult to mention them all here. Suffice it to say, several people provided assistance, challenge, and insight at various and opportune moments, which stimulated our thoughts and work. *From Evolution to Eden* is a better book because of their valuable comments and criticisms.

Gregory J. Laughery is especially thankful to his wife Elizabeth (Lisby) and to their sons, Vincent, Alexander, and Lawrence for sharing in the journey.

George R. Diepstra owes a debt of gratitude to his wife Eileen and to their daughter Karen, for their unwavering support throughout this project.

PREFACE

Do the early chapters of Genesis speak into
today's world, and if so, how?

Or has their voice been drowned out by a chorus
of other voices, particularly those coming
from the natural sciences?

In the past, literal interpretations of the Genesis stories of creation and fall played a dominant role in determining the general
contours of Christian belief. But such an interpretive orientation
seems more tenuous than ever in light of our contemporary scientific knowledge. For example, science is painting an evolutionary
portrait of human nature, including the origins of religious belief
that strikes directly at the heart of Genesis 1-3. The world has
been so naturalized by science that it has practically turned science and theology into competing enterprises, or so it seems. At
the very least, this raises questions about how the biblical text and
theology can accommodate such a natural picture of the world.
Perhaps we should leave the door open to the possibility that science is taking the process of naturalization too far. These difficult
and unsettling discussions are the turbulent waters out of which
the present work was born.

The essays in this book set out to engage these questions and represent a unique collaboration between a scientist with expertise in biology and a theologian who is an authority on the work of Paul Ricoeur and the study of hermeneutics. Our different backgrounds allow us to investigate the many facets of the science and theology discussion from different angles. The scientific perspective focuses on the exploration of nature through observation, experimentation, and theory building, while the theological perspective develops a vision of the world that strongly takes into account God, the biblical text, and the ancient world that formed the backdrop for the biblical story. By combining these perspectives, we hope to forge a path forward that places science and theology in an interactive and cooperative role, opening up new possibilities for our interpretation of Genesis 1-3.

Where does one begin such a daunting task? Perhaps we can turn to the artistic world, where the meaning and mysteries of life are contemplated, explored, and expressed in an effort to illuminate complexity and uncover valid directions. The great Spanish architect Antoni Gaudi captures something of the spirit of our work when he says, "Those who look for the laws of Nature as a support for their new works collaborate with the creator." For Gaudi, it was critically important to read (interpret) both the book of nature and the biblical text to fully appreciate life. In other words, he promoted a spirit of cooperation between God and nature. The best expression of this partnership can be found in his unfinished masterpiece, la Sagrada Familia basilica in Barcelona. To see how Gaudi achieved this feat, we need to take a journey around and through the basilica.

As we approach the cathedral, we come face to face with a breathtaking array of colossal walls, spires, windows, and sculptures that appear to spring outward and upward toward the heavens. Found in this explosion of architectural angles and designs are representative scenes from the biblical narrative, including the nativity and passion. These relief sculptures are complemented by the portals of faith, hope, and charity. Gaudi designed the outside of the basilica as a stunning display of the unfolding drama of the biblical story, a story that brings us into contact with realms beyond the world around us, realms which evade our total and complete understanding.

Upon entering the basilica, the experience continues as we are immediately struck by the presence of great stone pillars that hauntingly ascend to a cavernous ceiling. The pillars give the sense of being surrounded by a series of massive tree trunks. Once the ceiling is reached, the effect is completed by the presence of branches that form a silhouette of leaves overhead. And then as we look beyond the stone forest, shades of color dance through the pillars. Gaudi created this effect by strategically positioning long strips of colored glass on the walls of the cathedral, as well as placing two large stained glass rose windows on either side of the head apse. When light filters through the stained glass, colors appear to bleed from one window to the next. The visitor might feel a powerful sense of transformation as the colors run the gamut from blue to green to yellow to brown and bits of red. This sense of change intensifies as the light in the room undergoes dramatic variations in step with the time of day and the movement of clouds. Thus, the architecture itself reflects an assortment of changes in the natural world. Through this kind of splendor inside the basilica, glimpses of sacred space are configured in all their wonder and beauty, and the interplay between nature, perception, and thoughtful expression come to a climax.

What can we learn from Gaudi? In a sense, the basilica symbolizes our need to construct a cathedral-like place in our thinking, where beliefs drawn from both biblical and natural sources can be in dialogue. And just as the basilica reflected changes in the outside world, so must our sacred thoughts be open to changes in our understanding of the world around us. This makes the task of constructing our own cognitive cathedral of thoughts, questions, and beliefs an ongoing affair that never comes to a complete end. Interestingly, the basilica seems to reflect this point of view. It still stands unfinished after almost one-hundred-and-fifty years of construction. These images, and the complexity they provoke, set the stage for the work that follows.

In preparing the material for this book from a series of papers previously published in academic journals, we decided to make only minimal changes. We have arranged the contents in chronological order, so that the overall flow of the book accurately reflects how our thoughts moved from one question to the next. By placing the papers together in a single source, we hope to tell our own story of how our thinking about Genesis 1-3 unfolded, as we allowed the biblical world to meet and interact with our scientifically informed world. Hopefully, this will give readers some insight into what we think are the important questions that need to be raised as we come to terms with how to interpret and apply Genesis 1-3 today. In other words, our picture of this dynamic interdisciplinary relationship is a porous one, inviting our questions and daring us to venture down a new interpretive path with willingness to encounter what we find along the way.

Ch. 1

The first chapter lays out a general strategy for approaching the interaction between science and theology. It places a great deal of significance on the central role that interpretation plays in both. Once this pivotal function of interpretation is recognized, we begin to explore the implications of our interpretive finitude. We dismiss strong polarizations that pit the theological side against the scientific side, as well as efforts to either completely separate the theological world from the scientific world or to merge them seamlessly together. These overly simplistic approaches often give rise to dominating structures called metanarratives. Metanarratives, according to our perspective, are impenetrable fortresses that try to call all the shots and overrule other disciplines. We

Metanarratives

critique this and show that metanarratives grant far too much authority to the cognitive skills of humans, so that neither science nor theology can assume this status.

We conclude that science and theology are best viewed and described as informers working within what others have called a wide reflective equilibrium. Not only does this create a space for negotiation between informers, but it also emphasizes that one of the main features of this equilibrium is that it is time-sensitive. In other words, as our knowledge of the world changes, so must our interpretations, biblical or otherwise. This approach seems most fruitful, but it means that the interaction between science and theology will have to incorporate elements of constructive tension and inevitable uncertainty. *Challenging to the fundamentalist language*

From here, we embark on a series of excursions into Genesis 1-3. Along the way, we frequently consult the work of Paul Ricoeur for helpful ideas, since he has had a profound influence on the study of interpretation (hermeneutics) and the study and function of fictional and biblical narratives. Both fields of study will be important for developing a sound understanding of early *Ch. 2* Genesis. We begin, in the second chapter, by looking at what unifies Genesis 1-3. How can these chapters, with their two quite different creation stories, form a coherent whole? In order to come to a conclusion on this question, we explore the text from several different angles. We look carefully at the ancient world that formed the fertile ground from which the Hebrew story of beginnings grew. Eventually, we move into poetics and narrative formation. It is with these tools that we develop the idea that early Genesis is a founding narrative for the nation of Israel. It becomes a counter story to the other stories of its time, as it stakes out Yahweh Elohim as the God who stands above all other gods.

We next contemplate the mystery of time itself and how it *Ch. 3* is captured in a text like Genesis 1-3. On one hand, early Genesis is a product of its time. On the other hand, early Genesis is a

"Early Genesis is not a hard, factual description of beginnings, but a dynamic story that can engage our changing portraits of nature."

text that speaks beyond its time, but not in the precise way that many Christians presume. By exploring the interrelationships of time and narrative, we continue to work out our time-sensitive approach for interpreting the world and the text. Put simply, our interpretations are subject to change as our knowledge of the world changes. We show that early Genesis is not a hard, factual description of beginnings, but a dynamic story that can engage our changing portraits of nature.

Ch. 4

Finally, we examine more specifically Genesis 2-3. This has been one of the most difficult texts to reconcile with evolution. But does this need to be the case? In our concluding chapter, we pour all our resources from our previous work into looking at this question, developing an approach to Genesis 2-3 that avoids pitting the text against our evolutionary history. The hermeneutical strategy that we develop is described as a possible world/founding narrative paradigm. This strategy allows us to look at both the world of Eden and our present one as two quite different worlds that need to be taken on their own terms to avoid carelessly combining them. By doing so, we open up a dynamic picture of new possibilities for understanding our place in the world and our unfolding relationship with God.

?

SCRIPTURE, SCIENCE AND HERMENEUTICS

The world is charged with the grandeur of God

Gerard Manley Hopkins – "God's Grandeur"

In 1954 Bernard Ramm published his challenging and provocative book *The Christian View of Science and Scripture.*[1] In a world that was increasingly dominated by scientific explanations, he was acutely aware of the need for the Christian community to seriously consider the claims of science.

How was a Christian to formulate the relationship between science and Scripture? As Ramm's account has it, many Christians had put undue emphasis on a notion of discontinuity, leaving no other recourse but to deny any continuity and to seek to defend, "a position that violently contradicted the findings of science."[2]

This regrettable state of affairs, in Ramm's estimation, should have been supplanted by a more interactive view, which in the final analysis would find no conflict between true science and Scripture.[3] Yet, where does ultimate authority concerning the interpretation of the world and the life in it reside: in the hands of science or in the pages of Scripture? Notions of resolution to this complex issue are marked by a long and variegated history, and have proliferated in recent times.

---

1 B. Ramm, *The Christian View of Science and Scripture*, Grand Rapids: Eerdmans, 1954.

2 Ibid., 23.

3 Ibid., 17-42, esp. 42. The first chapter of Ramm's book is entitled, "The Imperative Necessity of a Harmony of Christianity and Science."

Since the writing of *The Christian View of Science and Scripture* the urgency of this discussion has only been reinforced by the accelerating expansion of our knowledge of the natural world over the last fifty years. Any survey of the current landscape, comprised of a variety of perspectives, shows that we are confronted with the reality of a polyphonic discourse concerning the appropriate relationship between science and Scripture. In response to this problematic, a cacophony of voices can now be heard, marking such deliberations with a matrix-like complexity that results in a lack of any clear-cut consensus.

[margin: many voiced]
[margin: harsh discordance of sound]

Our aim in this chapter is not to undertake an evaluation of all the entries on the historical or contemporary register, but rather to focus on three significant objectives: first, to examine the rise of hermeneutics and its implications for this debate; second, to assess the all too frequent polarizations in the world of science and Scripture in light of a hermeneutical perspective; and third, to explore the hermeneutical implications of two contemporary solutions that have been put forward to function as tension resolvers in the science and Scripture dialogue. We shall conclude by proposing a trajectory that aims to give full countenance to the hermeneutical reality lodged within the contours of the interaction between science and Scripture.

Why Hermeneutics?

Hermeneutics, the act and art of interpretation, has taken a prominent role in our day. The sheer velocity of this advance is staggering. An interpretative dimension is now acknowledged to touch all disciplines and every area of life. In a relatively short period of time, we have moved from the fairly specific definition of hermeneutics as the interpretation of legal and biblical texts, to a general definition where hermeneutics is understood as relating to the operations of understanding the whole of life. Specific or regional interpretative ventures, in this case, are frequently subjugated to a universalizing perspective which is thought to incorporate all regional hermeneutics into a general hermeneutics that concurrently subordinates properly epistemological concerns to ontological preoccupations.[4]

As Antje Jackelén points out in a recent essay, hermeneutics is one of three significant challenges facing science and religion today. Hermeneutics is not just a method; says Jackelén, "it is about the nature of understanding itself."[5] While this ontological shift has significant merit and many scholars affirm the importance of a general hermeneutics, it remains essential, in our view, to re-regionalize hermeneutics through a focus on the text and the world.[6] Hermeneutics then is not merely concerned with the nature of understanding, but also with the movements of explanation (epistemology) and new understanding, which taken together set up a dialogic interpretative horizon between self, world and text. Characterized by its striking ubiquity and vital challenge, hermeneutics needs to be given due consideration in the seemingly intractable debate between science and Scripture.

We would argue, whether one is reading the natural world or the biblical text, both enterprises are interpretative ventures with varying degrees of objectivity. Scientists and biblical interpreters, that is, are on common hermeneutical ground: a hermeneutics of finitude. This means that they each find themselves grounded within interpretative and overlapping frameworks from which neither can extract themselves in order to make the claim to having a neutral objective standpoint.[7] The old adage that scientists

---

4   P. Ricoeur, *From Text to Action, Essays in Hermeneutics, II*, trans., K. Blamey and J. B. Thompson, Evanston: Northwestern University Press, 1991, 53-101.

5   A. Jackelén, "Science and Religion: Getting Ready for the Future," *Zygon* 38, no. 2 (June 2003), 210.

6   Ricoeur, *From Text to Action*, 53-101. This movement of hermeneutical re-regionalization is one of the major motifs in Ricoeur's work.

7   Ibid., 54. Ricoeur states, "Indeed, hermeneutics itself puts us on guard against the illusion or pretention of neutrality."

are uninvolved observers and that science is solely about the facts has been undergoing serious reassessment, and rightly so, since at least the days of Polanyi and Kuhn.[8] An equally significant and judicious challenge is taking place with respect to biblical readers who have also embraced their own myths of impartiality in assuming that they read the Bible as solely a book of facts with no need of interpretation.

The growing emphasis on hermeneutics is important at several levels, but for the purposes of our discussion, it is at least significant in the following way: Scientific and biblical interpretation are both produced by humans who have finite interpretative contexts and whose understanding, explanation, and new understanding are hermeneutical, having the capacity to create suspicion,[9] counter dogmatism, and check reductionism.[10]

A hermeneutics of finitude and suspicion, for example, begins to make us aware of our own situatedness, offers a critique of any notion of a view from no-where, and provides the necessary trajectory towards a robust hermeneutics of trust. Those who read the natural world and those who read Scripture have not always adequately considered the force of this developing hermeneutical revolution on their reflections. That is, there is a fair amount of hermeneutically mis-informed rhetoric on both sides of this debate, which often trenchantly insists on a divide - and - conquer perspective. Embracing such an outlook results in polarized points of view, which in turn ignore or discount the gravity of a hermeneutical trajectory.

---

8 M. Polanyi, *Personal Knowledge: Towards a Post-Critical Philosophy*, Chicago: The University of Chicago Press, 1958. T. S. Kuhn, *The Structure of Scientific Revolutions*, Second Edition, Chicago: The University of Chicago Press, 1970.

9 M. Westphal, *Suspicion & Faith: The Religious uses of Modern Atheism*, Grand Rapids: Eerdmans, 13, in commenting on the masters of suspicion - Marx, Nietzsche, and Freud - refers to a hermeneutics of suspicion this way: "the deliberate attempt to expose the self-deceptions involved in hiding our actual operative motives from ourselves, individually and collectively, in order not to notice how and how much our behavior and our beliefs are shaped by values we profess to disown."

10 See Ricoeur, "Science and Ideology," in *Hermeneutics and the Human Sciences*, trans., and edited by J. B. Thompson, Cambridge: Cambridge University Press, 1981, 222-246.

For some in the natural sciences this means there is little or no place for the biblical text.[11] For a number of biblical interpreters this means a paltry or inconsequential recognition of the value of science with respect to the interpretation of life and the world.[12] There are many biblical interpreters who tenaciously refuse to consider scientific interpretations of the natural world, while many in the scientific community adamantly ignore biblical interpretations of the same world.

A re-regionalized hermeneutics that acknowledges the natural world and Scripture are credible and crucial hermeneutical factors that demand careful consideration for understanding and explaining something of life as we know it. Hermeneutically speaking, therefore, we contend that the biblical text and the natural world should be given their appropriate places as legitimate informers in the act and art of the interpretation of life in the world.

The reality of a hermeneutical perspective then, if we are willing to acknowledge it, begins to challenge us to consider possibilities that may not fall within the scope of more narrow, even at times reductionistic, knowledge frameworks. Hermeneutics is a common ground dynamic that aligns ways of understanding, opens up possibilities for explaining life in the world, and leads potentially to new understanding, be it scientific or biblical. At the same time, hermeneutics confronts those in both fields of inquiry with the truth that they not only read and interpret, but that they are also being read and interpreted by the data with which they interact.

Furthermore, a hermeneutical trajectory is one that it is obliged to incorporate reader, text and world. There is an inevitable, but not always noticed, motion here: from the reader, through the subject matter of inquiry and investigation (world/text), and then

---

11 C. Westermann, *Creation*, trans., J. J. Scullion, Philadelphia: Fortress, 1974 , 3ff.

12 N. Saunders, Divine Action and Modern Science, Cambridge: Cambridge University Press, 2002, x-xi.

back to the reader.[13] As readers, we start with some understanding of ourselves and the world. Through interaction with the text/world, this understanding is explained, and in many instances either affirmed or critiqued, en route to new understanding. A hermeneutics in motion refutes the image of a vicious circle, embracing in its place the triadic symbol of productive dialogue between reader, text and world. Hence one's understanding, explanation, and new understanding of the world can be viewed as a dynamic process that consists of an ongoing dialogue comprised of a spiraling resonance between these entities.

Science as Informer

Knowledge of our world is marked by degrees of complexity and uncertainty. Resolution of the uncertainty factor frequently becomes a dominant theme within the contours of the overall debate concerning valid informers. For many scientists, denouement is a matter of assigning an authoritative voice to the knowledge acquired from scientific endeavors. Reinforced by the sheer magnitude of the growing knowledge bank concerning natural phenomena, this perspective promotes an understanding and interpretation of the world and the life found within it that is restricted to empirical investigation.

In a recent publication, the image of science as a "candle in the dark" was employed to help convey the sense of enlightenment that scientific knowledge has conferred upon our understanding of the world.[14] Not only has this candle added to our understanding, but scientific reflection has also deconstructed many of our preconceived notions of the world. The growing realization of a complex and diverse Earth history and the corresponding advent

13 G. J. Laughery, *Living Hermeneutics in Motion: An Analysis and Evaluation of Paul Ricoeur's Contribution to Biblical Hermeneutics*, Lanham: University Press of America, 2002.

14 C. Sagan, *The Demon-Haunted World: Science as a Candle in the Dark*, New York: Ballantine Books, 1996.

of geological science in the nineteenth century, for example, disrupted the prevailing medieval notion of a brief static picture of the world. This static view, which emerged out of the synthesis of biblical interpretation and Greek thought, gradually gave way to a dynamic view that pictured Earth history as a long succession of events.[15] Soon thereafter, scientific investigation of the heavens led to a similar recognition of the dynamic nature of stellar and galactic history.[16]

This often-cited example of growing scientific awareness serves to illustrate that the exploration of nature can result in a major shift in our interpretative vision of the world. Such a successful and powerful shift in perspective can have at least two significant outcomes. First, it can provoke a variety of responses ranging from assimilation to hostility depending on the variables of the context. Second, it can create the illusory sense that scientific discoveries and their derivative concepts dominate the hermeneutical landscape.

There are some in the scientific community who adopt this dominating perspective and assign a definitive informing role to the natural sciences. Operating within the confines of a materialistic framework, the result is an ever-widening circle of explanatory power that infuses a naturalistic orientation into other realms of thought from ethics[17] to sociology.[18] This perspective typically produces a grand scheme in which the inevitable tensions that develop between disciplines are viewed as theoretically tractable by utilizing the tools of material science. The fundamental role of the

---

15 D. A. Young, "The Discovery of Terrestrial History," in *Portraits of Creation: Biblical and Scientific Perspectives on the World's Formation*, H. J. Van Till, R. E. Snow, J. H. Stek, and D. A. Young, Grand Rapids: Eerdmans, 1990, 26-81.

16 H. J. Van Till, "The Scientific Investigation of Cosmic History," in *Portraits of Creation*, 82-84.

17 M. Ruse and E. O. Wilson, "The Approach of Sociobiology: The Evolution of Ethics," in: *Religion and the Natural Sciences: The Range of Engagement*, J. E. Huchingson, ed., Orlando: Harcourt Brace, 1993, 308-311.

18 E. O. Wilson, *Sociobiology: the New Synthesis*, Cambridge: Harvard Univ. Press, 1975.

natural sciences then becomes the simplest and best route toward reducing the uncertainties of our understanding and explanation of the world. Edward O. Wilson exemplifies a comprehensive commitment to scientific materialism. In his book *Consilience*, Wilson clearly articulates his materialistic vision when he states:

> I have argued that there is intrinsically only one class of explanation. There is abundant evidence to support and none absolutely to refute the proposition that consilient explanations are congenial to the entirety of the great branches of learning. The central idea of the consilience world view is that all tangible phenomena, from the birth of stars to the workings of social institutions, are based on material processes that are ultimately reducible, however long and tortuous the sequences, to the laws of physics. [19]

This ontological reductionism breeds an epistemological reductionism that permeates all other segments of learning. The term *consilience* in this context implies a linking of facts and fact-based theory across disciplines in order to create a common groundwork of explanation. Accordingly, any fragmentation of knowledge is viewed as an artifact of scholarship and is resolvable by operating upon the conviction that the world is orderly and can be completely explained at the level of natural category.[20]

In Wilson's approach, scientific naturalism is hermeneutically stretched so that once something, including social behaviors like religion, can be explained by material causes it is thereby concluded that the entity in question must be a completely material phenomenon.[21] From our point of view, this use of evolutionary descriptions is an example of how scientific information can be

---

19 E. O. Wilson, *Consilience*, New York: Knopf, 1998, 266.

20 Ibid., 4, 8. A fair question, under hermeneutical considerations, relates to whether this kind of interpretative exclusivity is itself an artifact of scholarship; notably Wilson's.

21 E. O. Wilson, *On Human Nature*, Cambridge, MA: Harvard Univ. Press, 1978, 192. See C. O. Schrag, *The Self After Postmodernity*, New Haven: Yale University Press, 1997, 118-127, for a stimulating discussion of the role of religion in Kant and Kierkegaard.

hardened into an inviolable naturalistic informer that closes constructive engagement with other informing sources.

Aside from technical questions as to the role of material causes in Wilson's grand explanation, he never adequately contends with the idea that the religious impulse might engender other explanations. [22] Kenneth Miller, by contrast, in a less reductionistic fashion, queries whether it is possible that evolutionary processes might be the means by which "a Deity ensured His message found receptive ground."[23] Wilson's scientism excludes any such possibility.

Similar types of thinking pervade the work of various contemporary writers.[24] Details may vary, but the same general theme prevails: humans can attain epistemological certainty by adopting a dominating role for the informing capacity of the natural sciences. The remarks of chemist Peter Atkins herald the triumph of this line of thought when he states:

> Religion has failed, and its failures should be exposed. Science, with its currently successful pursuit of universal competence through the identification of the minimal, the supreme delight of the intellect, should be acknowledged king.[25]

Has science suddenly become hermeneutically immunized against failure? Why is the success of science a measure of completion? Even the resources of philosophy are subject to these influences as they are recruited to unify our knowledge under this representa-

---

22 K. R. Miller, *Finding Darwin's God: A Scientist's Search for Common Ground Between God and Evolution*, New York: HarperCollins, 1999, 182-183.

23 Ibid., 183.

24 See D. Dennett, *Darwin's Dangerous Idea: Evolution and the Meanings of Life*, New York: Simon & Schuster, 1995, 21; R. Dawkins, *The Blind Watchmaker: Why the evidence of evolution reveals a universe without design*, New York: W.W. Norton, 1987, 13-15 and F. Crick, *The Astonishing Hypothesis: The Scientific Search for the Soul*, New York: Scribner, 1994, 3.

25 P. Atkins, "The Limitless Power of Science," in *Nature's Imagination: The Frontiers of Scientific Vision*, J. Cornwell, ed., Oxford: Oxford Univ. Press, 1995, 132.

tive paradigm.[26] Thus, the search for a coherent explanation of the world is envisioned by giving strong assent to an exclusionary method of unification.

Inevitably, this perspective negates any significant role for religion in informing our current understanding and explanation of the world. In Wilsonian style, the primary merit of religion is often reduced to the idea that it has functioned as a valuable survival mechanism based on its ability to facilitate group cohesion.[27] But even if this accurately portrays one aspect of religion, does the acceptance of such a position dogmatically announce a significant diminution in the role theological insight plays in our understanding and explanation of the world? When these naturalistic concepts are wielded in the grasp of scientific materialism, the answer is yes. The authoritative voice of any traditional religious community is silenced by reducing it to a mere product of evolution. Ian Barbour notes that in Wilson's judgment, the functions that were performed by religion in the past are now better served by a "poetic rendition of the evolutionary epic."[28] Acknowledging the human propensity and need to devise sacred narratives, this evolutionary epic is transformed into metanarrative: a grandiose story of mythological proportions configured as the scientific dismantler of the ancient mythic stories.[29]

It is not our intention in this brief overview to analyze the details of this type of conjecture, nor to dismiss the scientific conclusions contained therein. Our aim is rather to draw attention to the totalizing perspective that has been adopted. There is no question that our scientific knowledge has been instrumental in challenging many of our beliefs and has served to sharpen our

---

26 Dennett, *Freedom Evolves*, New York: Viking, 2003, 15.

27 I. G. Barbour, *When Science Meets Religion*, New York: HarperCollins, 2000, 13.

28 Ibid., 156.

29 E. O. Wilson, *On Human Nature*, 191-192.

thoughts across many disciplines. However, we are concerned that effectual critique has been so severely hampered by narrowing the scope of the dialogue that scientific thought has been freed to go about creating its own set of illusions.

Our objective, at this juncture, is to pursue two lines of thought that more clearly articulate our perspective of science as informer. We will draw upon philosophy and then history. First, since the view of scientific rationality described above can be characterized as modernist,[30] the insights of a postmodern analysis of knowledge may warrant consideration.[31] In his thought provoking volume, *The Postmodern Condition: A Report on Knowledge,* Jean-François Lyotard exposes the problematic nature of the exclusivity claims of scientific knowledge. He states:

> In the first place, scientific knowledge does not represent the totality of knowledge; it has always existed in addition to, and in competition and conflict with, another kind of knowledge, which I will call narrative in the interests of simplicity.[32]

Lyotard has argued, among other things, that the postmodern is to be defined as "incredulity towards metanarratives."[33] He contends that metanarratives, a feature of modernism, exist in order to legitimate their own knowledge, interests and practices.[34] Metanarratives, therefore, crystallize a totalizing perspective - story-ing a

---

30 See J. W. van Huyssteen, *The Shaping of Rationality: Toward Interdisciplinarity in Theology and Science,* Grand Rapids: Eerdmans, 1999, 237.

31 A. Jackelén, "Science and Religion: Getting Ready for the Future," 210, rightly argues that postmodernisms are another significant challenge to the discussion of science and religion.

32 J.-F. Lyotard, *The Postmodern Condition: A Report on Knowledge,* trans., G. Bennington and B. Massumi, Minneapolis: University of Minnesota Press, 1984, 7. See also, J. Baudrillard, *The Perfect Crime,* trans., C. Turner, London: Verso, 1996, for a discussion of consensus and closure.

33 Ibid., xxiv. Lyotard's version of postmodernism, however, does not rule out *mega-narratives = Big narratives.* We express our gratitude to Merold Westphal for the notion of *mega* versus *meta.*

34 Ibid., xxiii.

theory of Everything in an attempt to construct explanatory invincibility. Invincibility can be assured by a power play that deprives other potentially valid informers, external to the scientific one, of any credibility. Clearly, based on this definition the vision of science mentioned above qualifies as metanarrative.

An awareness of the potential self-interest and self-deception configured within one's discipline is heightened by the practice of a hermeneutics of finitude and of suspicion. When this awareness is coupled with a postmodern critique of metanarrative, any over-arching meta (scientific or otherwise), in its presumptuous attempt to fulfill the demands for total epistemological closure, becomes transparent as an illusory symbol.[35] In our opinion, as we grope for optimal explanation, this dimension of postmodernism along with a note of suspicion, needs to be taken into account if we are to avert the tyranny of perceived explanatory closure by an over-zealous scientific informer.

Following the postmodern direction of Lyotard, Joseph Rouse introduces the notion of cultural studies of the sciences. The sciences are envisioned as, "cultural formations that must be understood through a detailed examination of the resources on which their articulation draws, the situations to which they respond, and the ways they transform those situations and have an impact on others."[36] Among other things, this perspective implies that scientific work should exhibit a degree of openness that consists of currents that flow between the sciences and the rest of culture. The distinction between what is scientific and what is not is thereby destabilized to some extent.[37]

---

35 At any rate, whether or not closure can be or has been achieved is not a question that can be answered by simply structuring the question within the boundaries of empirically based scientific knowledge. See also Ricoeur, *The Symbolism of Evil*, trans., E. Buchanan, New York: Harper & Row, 1967; Boston: Beacon, 1969, 347-357. Symbols, according to Ricoeur, should give rise to thought and be understood as an augmentation of reality, not a closure of it.

36 J. Rouse, *Engaging Science: How to Understand Its Practices Philosophically*, Ithaca: Cornell Univ. Press, 1996, 239.

37 Ibid., 249-250.

J. Wentzel van Huyssteen offers a helpful analysis of Rouse's work concerning the relationship between theology and science. Recognizing that Rouse adopts a narrow definition of postmodernism as a mindset to be overcome, rather than as a tool with which to critically evaluate modernity, van Huyssteen acknowledges Rouse's important contribution to the rejection of any grand narrative scheme of science. The inability to uphold sharp distinctions between the empirical and the interpretative dimensions opens the door for a wider reflective movement.[38] In our estimation, the interpretative dimension should be widened, and a more porous concept of science as informer needs to be set in motion to counter the hubris of scientific over-determination.

To reinforce this idea we briefly turn to a second line of thought: the history of science. At the end of his stimulating book, *A History of Western Science*, Anthony Alioto concludes that the so-called scientific outlook is an illusion and that science is a cultural artifact that belongs to the West.[39] Although this may sound a bit severe, what is suggested by these comments is the recognition that the discoveries of science emanate from the total human matrix. As a matrix, it involves "the extremely complex interplay of aesthetics, values, religion, passions" in interaction with the physical world.[40] In this sense, every observation is a dialogue that eludes a tight prescriptive net and thereby invites a more inclusive approach to our explanation and understanding of the world.[41]

A more focused examination of both science and religion from a historical perspective led John Hedley Brooke to the realization that the boundaries between "science" and "religion" have shifted over time and therefore, abstracting some correct and timeless view

---

38 van Huyssteen , *The Shaping of Rationality*, 33-55.

39 A. Alioto, *A History of Western Science*, Englewood Cliffs: Prentice Hall, 1993, 441.

40 Ibid., 441.

41 P. Feyerabend, *Against Method*, London: Verso, 1975, 214, questions whether science as we know it could have even arisen within the "blunt application of 'rational' procedures."

of these entities is problematic.[42] In the past, for example, it was common to encounter scientific pioneers whose science was strongly informed by theological and metaphysical beliefs.[43] This does not mean that those with such beliefs had free reign to discount scientific concepts, but it does draw into question the validity of an over-determining version of science. Brooke concludes from his historical survey that theories are under-determined by supporting data and that "aesthetic and religious beliefs have played a selective role in the past."[44] This perspective raises a fair challenge to the notion that scientific knowledge can be abstracted into a definitive interpretative vehicle that comprises our total understanding of the world in the quest for epistemological certainty.

Since tight prescriptive definitions of science are elusive, it may be helpful to note what science is not. Science does not attempt to include divine causes in its explanations of the natural world, nor does it necessarily attempt to refute them.[45] This exclusionary principle may serve to delimit scientific objectives, but it fails to extract science from contextual and hermeneutical influences. Furthermore, there are common points of contact in the world where both science and religion have a vested interest, as we will note later, so that any notion of clean separation at the interpretative level is impossible.

It is important to point out that it was not our objective in this section to give a comprehensive description of what science is, but rather to challenge the modernist tendency to rationalize science as an exclusive way of knowing that provides certainty.

---

42 J. H. Brooke, *Science and Religion: Some Historical Perspectives,* Cambridge: Cambridge University Press, 1991, 8, draws attention to the fact that both are human endeavors subject to human concerns. On p. 42 he concludes that both are complex social activities and that their interaction cannot be structured in any simple formulation (51).

43 Ibid., 19.

44 Ibid., 327.

45 J. A. Moore, *Science as a Way of Knowing: The Foundations of Modern Biology*, Cambridge, MA: Harvard Univ Press, 1993, 502.

With this in mind, why have we chosen the term informer to apply to science? In our thinking, the concept of informer includes several general features. As we have affirmed, scientific studies clearly have made vital additions and readjustments to our knowledge about the world and ourselves. In terms of a way of knowing, modern science relies on observation, experimentation and the integration of data into coherent explanations about many aspects and features of the natural world.[46] While confirming the strong empirical footing of scientific thinking, we contend that it is equally important to view scientific endeavors as human endeavors embedded in the world that scientists seek to explain. Hence, scientific conclusions are often tentative and subject to the type of hermeneutical considerations mentioned above.

It is not our intention to eschew the weighty findings of scientists like E. O. Wilson. Sociobiology, for example, has made major contributions to our understanding of animal behavior and needs to be seriously considered.[47] However, while we can agree with these scientific insights, our brief postmodern and historical analysis points us beyond a Wilsonian interpretative framework that sanctions a total domination by the natural sciences.

In concluding our remarks about science as informer we claim that any attempt to abstract and absolutize our scientific knowledge is implausible. In his seminal work, Michael Polanyi concluded that, "science is a system of beliefs to which we are committed ... and points beyond itself in the direction of a fiduciary formulation of science."[48] From our point of view, this implies the convergence of science and hermeneutics at the epistemological level. It is crucial to note that from a hermeneutical perspective, our scientific endeavors involve a continuous motion between the

---

46 Ibid., 503.

47 See J. Alcock, *The Triumph of Sociobiology*, Oxford: Oxford University Press, 2001.

48 Polanyi, *Personal Knowledge*, 171.

world and one's understanding and explanation of the world that leads to new understanding.[49] This encounter not only shapes one's knowledge of the world, but it shapes one as the knower of that world. Thus, it is of paramount importance that the scientific informer be positioned within the contours of a broad hermeneutical context that leaves the search for understanding and explaining the world open and that counters the overindulgence of empirical conclusions which tend to create a false sense of certainty. With these considerations in mind, we turn to examine Scripture as informer.

Scripture as Informer

Many in theological circles advocate an inordinately determinative role for the scriptural text when interpreting the natural world. As the text works on the world and the world works on the text, through the mediation of the reader, Scripture is thought to empower the reader by strongly sculpting knowledge about the world. Theological positions that espouse some form of biblical literalism tend to weight Scripture to the fullest extent in this interaction. In these cases, the biblical text often functions as a fact-laden resource that yields precise information about the natural world.

Undergirding this approach is an implicit often unrecognized epistemology: knowledge is pristinely rational, crystal clear and fully objective. As this epistemology is granted unquestionably free access to a biblical text that is configured as a transparent book of facts and evidences about God and the world, the text attains an elevated position of final arbiter in a variety of discussions. This epistemological-textual model leads to a fitting response: proving that creation attests to a set of particular dogmatic perspectives concerning the way the natural world was and

---

49 See Laughery, *Living Hermeneutics in Motion*, for a fuller discussion of hermeneutical motion.

is and must be. Acquiescence to this totalizing perspective framed within the strictures of biblical literalism generates a sense of certainty that can dictate scientific conclusions.[50] Not surprisingly, quasi-theological inventions like scientific creationism are spawned from this kind of theological chemistry, -- inventions that frequently find themselves at odds with prevailing currents in the academic world.

The roots of this type of perspective can be traced back to the marked influence of an enlightenment epistemology on some forms of Christian thought at the turn of the eighteenth century.[51] Overtly represented in dispensational views, the scientific and objective character of theology was defended as the theological ideal.[52] Typical of this theological accommodation to a scientific approach are the comments of the dispensationalist Arthur T. Pierson at the end of the nineteenth century. Pierson advocated a Baconian system that gathered the facts from Scripture in order to deduce general laws for organizing those facts.[53] In other words, Scripture was viewed as an encyclopedic jigsaw puzzle that should be subjected to an intensive inductive approach in order to uncover and unify the hard facts.[54]

The residue from this period persists in the mindset of many present day Christians. They are committed to a particular notion of epistemology, often linked to modernism, and a "scientific approach" to Scripture.[55] Accordingly, Scripture is used to generate knowledge about the natural world and to regulate our understanding of this world. Frequently, this interpretative disposition

---

50 Barbour, *When Science Meets Religion*, 16.

51 M. Noll, *The Scandal of the Evangelical Mind*, Grand Rapids: Eerdmans, 1994, 83.

52 Ibid., 127

53 G. Marsden, *Fundamentalism and American Culture: The Shaping of Twentieth-Century Evangelicalism: 1870-1925*, Oxford: Oxford University Press, 1980, 55.

54 Ibid., 58-59.

55 Noll, *The Scandal of the Evangelical Mind*, 83.

is linked to a configuration of Scripture as the carrier of God's specific, unimpeachable information about the structure and formation of the world. This perspective aligns Scripture in direct confrontation with various scientific conclusions.[56] All too often the result is a form of theological reductionism that strongly favors a view of Scripture as exclusive world informer and that tends to close off many potentially valid insights from other informers, such as science. Although the severity of this closure is variable, the tendency is to initially place many controversial issues, like evolutionary thinking, into the category of a dispute between worldviews and, thereby, intensify the closure.[57]

From this brief sketch of a perspective that dogmatically and narrowly applies Scripture to our understanding of the world emanate several comments relevant to our framing of Scripture as an informer. We begin by noting that theological movements with modernist overtones tend toward a totalizing perspective for Scripture's role in our understanding and interpretation of the world and are vulnerable to the same metanarrative criticism leveled against an exaggerated scientific informer. Although it may be fair to say that Scripture has a more global and synthetic approach to life, a topic to which we will return shortly, this does not necessarily imply that Scripture can or should be thought to speak in a definitive explanatory manner at every turn in the discussion.

Several problems result from the attempt to achieve certainty and a strong measure of explanatory closure by sifting and assem-

---

56 Ibid., 201-202. Noll quotes J. C. Whitcomb, Jr. and H. M. Morris from *The Genesis Flood: The Biblical Record and Its Scientific Implications*, Philadelphia: Presbyterian and Reformed, 1961, as representative of an instinctive trust in the perspicuity of Scripture and the ability to clearly align scientific data within the biblical framework in a way that may necessitate significant modifications in the scientific picture of the world.

57 This has taken on current significance by many individuals supporting the intelligent design motif. See, for example, W. Dembski, *Intelligent Design: The Bridge Between Science & Theology*, Downers Grove: Intervarsity Press, 1999, 114, 120 and P. Johnson, *Reason in the Balance: The Case Against NATURALISM in Science, Law & Education*, Downers Grove: Intervarsity Press, 1995, 7-17.

bling answers out of the biblical text. First, this type of scriptural informer, as was the case with an excessive scientific informer, can develop a false sense of invincibility that unduly hastens to close the channels of dialogue and critique. This situation, as we pointed out previously, is subject to a strong note of suspicion and reconsideration on the grounds of a hermeneutical analysis.

Closure, within this stream of Christian thought, has always been most vigorously pursued regarding perspectives of the world that incorporate an evolutionary framework. However, despite the fact that the evolutionary paradigm has often been co-opted and employed to support a materialistic outlook, many Christian thinkers have considered it possible, if not preferred, to accept evolution as the best description of many features of the natural world. This was the case at the time of Darwin among some lead-ing Christian thinkers in both scientific and theological circles, such as Asa Gray and B. B. Warfield respectively,[58] as well as with a variety of thinkers since. In a recent book that consists of a series of essays by orthodox Christians, for example, a compelling case is presented for considering the configuration of the natural world to be that of an evolving creation.[59]

Another problem that arises from attempts at tight explana-tory closure with Scripture is related to the idea that there is an unequal distribution of information between informers. The en-gagement of Scripture in the dynamics of interpreting our world is restricted in the sense that as a completed text, its content is fixed in quantity. Consequently, as our scientific knowledge of the world grows and confronts our theological thinking, Scripture is summoned into the role of a respondent. As such, theological in-

---

58 D. Livingstone, *Darwin's Forgotten Defenders: The Encounter Between Evangelical Theology and Evolutionary Thought*, Vancouver: Regent College Publishing, 1984, 60-64, 119, 146-147.

59 In K. B. Miller, ed., *Perspectives on an Evolving Creation*, Grand Rapids: Eerdmans, 2003, an assortment of articles from authors across a variety of disciplines has been compiled in support of the assessment that evolutionary configurations of creation are compatible with orthodox, evangelical Christianity.

novations ranging from a strict creationism to the integration of process thought in the theology/science discussion are incubated and born as products of theological reflection. Any notion of simply lifting the "facts" directly from the text is strongly challenged as due consideration is given to both the interpretative dimensions of this procedure and the multi-factorial nature of it.

In our opinion, a more productive approach to our considerations of Scripture as an informer may be found in the elaboration of the idea that the theological perspective implies a radical redescription of the world.[60] Niels Gregersen contends that this redescription involves the interpretation of existence and not simply the interpretation of the text. Stating that a common interest in life processes is shared by theological and biological concerns, he notes that their conceptions of life are not coextensive in that theology is not only concerned with how the world is, but with what it could and should become. Gregersen further notes that this redescription illuminates our understanding of the world in a way "that allows us to see more than it would otherwise be possible to see without this redescription."[61] In our view, this redescription encompasses both the interpretation of existence and the reorientation of existence in a biblically informed manner. Such a comprehensive, theologically based worldview it not only counters scientific reductionism,[62] but rightly draws into question the assumed merits of a theological reductionism that empowers Scripture to over-describe the natural world, and in so doing, excessively isolate scriptural knowledge. As van Huyssteen has noted "our scientific understanding of the world is indeed capable of both limiting and expanding the worldview offered by a theological description."[63]

---

60 van Huyssteen, *Duet or Duel? Theology and Science in a Postmodern World*, Harrisburg: Trinity Press International, 1998, 83.

61 N. Gregersen, "Theology in a Neo-Darwinian World," *Studia Theologica* 48 (1994), 125-126.

62 van Huyssteen, *Duet or Duel?*, 161.

63 Ibid., 161.

Integral to this process, then, is a vibrant resonance between our engagement with the unfolding knowledge of the world, the interpretation of the biblical text in light of that knowledge, and the theological redescription of the world that is precipitated by this interaction. Viewed as a circuitous motion proceeding to and from this theological redescription, there is an ongoing dialogue and negotiation between the scientific and theological spheres of influence. As Hans Schwarz points out:

> Since Christian faith is lived in this world and in our present history, the findings of science can be used to illustrate the Christian faith in God the creator, sustainer, and redeemer. In order to do justice to science, this cannot be done by usurping scientific findings for theological purposes, but must take place in continuous dialogue with scientists and their findings.[64]

This more open encounter functions in an interpretative space where agreement, conflict and uncertainty co-exist. Consequently, the entire interpretive movement is inherently fraught with constructive tension. Within this context, Scripture becomes the volatile ingredient in the interpretive mixture that provokes a reorienting redescription of the world in a way that can direct and challenge our comprehensive theorizing about the world. Implied in this interpretive resonance is a less competitive posture toward scientific conclusions with the recognition that a thorough going resolution between our scientific reflections and theological reflections is often elusive. Simply adopting a stance where the scriptural informer is more exclusionary only serves to place it in a strong disjunctive posture with our knowledge of the world and artificially limits the dimensions of this interpretive motion. By exploiting this type of hermeneutical reductionism, an illusionary sense of tension resolution between Scripture and our knowledge of the natural world is created.

---

64 H. Schwarz, *Creation*, Grand Rapids: Eerdmans, 2002, 241.

In conclusion, it is important to note that the biblical text is framed within an ancient cultural context and employs phenomenal language in its descriptions, particularly in regions of the text that most directly impact our scientific images. Interpreting these selective passages as scientific propositions about the world is a highly suspect maneuver. The fact that many in religious circles have been quick to do so only reinforces the conclusion that they have been strongly impacted by a modernist sense of scientific domination.[65] This influence routinely leads to the development of an interpretive consciousness that equates epistemic value in these passages with scientific content. However, by framing Scripture's informing role within the contours of an interpretive motion that incorporates and adjusts a theological redescription of the world, it promotes the de-coupling of the scriptural informer from the hubris of overly specifying a particular scientific configuration of the world. As this concerted movement passes down the corridors of time, Scripture is free from the constraints of over-description and is able to contend with the changing scientific configurations of the world in an open and reorienting fashion. In this sense, Scripture's informing role is as valid in our present context as it was in so called "pre-scientific" times.

Integration or Complementarity?

The previous two sections have reviewed the type of resolution between science and theology that is achieved by adopting procedures of exclusivity and domination. One of the points we noted was that when either the scientific or scriptural informer is dislodged from a wider interpretative framework, over-determination and excessive conflict become likely outcomes. In this

---

65 C. Hyers, *The Meaning of Creation: Genesis and Modern Science*, Atlanta: John Knox Press, 1984, 29-33, 37-56 points out that how the universe is conceptually organized (37) is not the preeminent concern of Scripture, but rather that the vast array of phenomena, however they are organized, "are the objects of divine creation and sovereignty." See also H. Blocher, *In the Beginning: The Opening Chapters of Genesis*, Downers Grove: Intervarsity Press, 1984, 15-78.

atmosphere of conflict, the scientific and scriptural informers vie for hermeneutical/epistemological supremacy.

A variety of solutions have been posited to address this problematic. Often both informers are incorporated to a greater extent in an interpretation of the world, yet with a modicum of disharmony between them. At the risk of oversimplification, these *tension resolvers* may be divided into two categories: integration and complementarity. We shall begin with a brief description of an integrative program that embraces process thought in order to question whether collapsing our scientific and scriptural knowledge into such an integrative whole will result in a diminution in interpretive tension without diminishing the integrity of one of the informers.

Ian Barbour summarizes the comprehensive nature of process thought when he states "process philosophy has developed a systematic metaphysics that is consistent with the evolutionary, many-leveled view of nature." Indebted to process thought's analogy between the world and an organism with the attending idea that the world is a community of events, Barbour goes on to note that reality can best be interpreted as "an interacting network of individual *moments of experience*."[66] Difficulties arise, however, concerning the open-endedness of these experiences and whether enough weight is given to the temporality and telos of reality.

When this system is integrated with theology, God becomes circumscribed in a more open relational world where He not only is strongly influenced by the events of the world, but His influence in the events of the world is persuasive in nature rather than coercive. God's persuasive interaction with the world, then, is configured as lures that prompt events toward idealized outcomes that result in the actualization of particular potentialities.[67] Thus,

---

[66] Barbour, *Religion in an Age of Science*, San Francisco: HarperCollins, 1990, 221, 223.

[67] Ibid., 231.

God's interaction with the world is often reduced to that of a relatively passive pleader at the margins of the world.[68]

With these brief remarks in mind, it seems appropriate to raise the query of whether the use of process thinking in the science and theology discussion is too strongly governing the interpretive voice of one or both of our informers. A number of objections to the process vision of the world have been raised at both the scientific and theological levels. John Polkinghorne, for example, disputes the idea that the physical world exhibits the "discrete graininess" implicit in process thought, and barbs at the process world as bordering on a panpsychic view of reality.[69] Ian Barbour raises the question of "whether human experience has such a fragmentary and episodic character." Furthermore, he doubts whether the Whiteheadian system can adequately account for the diverse activity at varying levels of organization, as well as the occurrence of novelty throughout evolutionary history. We would agree with Barbour's assessment, but not with his contention that process thinking can be modified to accommodate these issues.[70] In our judgment, an appropriate response at this juncture would be to challenge the integrative practices of any grand scale speculative philosophy, like process thought, on the grounds that it can lead to a form of hermeneutical reductionism that compromises the acumen of both the scientific and scriptural informers.

The objections to this kind of comprehensive integration are only compounded when the theological implications are considered. This is particularly acute when process theologians like Charles Hartshorne ensnare the redemptive event in the process net. Malcolm Jeeves and R.J. Berry note that as Christian theology, process theology "is seriously defective because it relegates

---

68 J. Polkinghorne, *Reason and Reality: The Relationship between Science & Theology*, Philadelphia: Trinity Press International, 1991, 47.

69 Polkinghorne, *Belief in God in an Age of Science*, New Haven: Yale University Press, 1998, 56.

70 Barbour, *Religion in an Age of Science*, 227.

Christ's death to a mere catalyst within history, and empties it of all eternal significance." When they examine concepts like panentheism, which is often assimilated by process theologians, they contend that it is not based on Scripture, but rather depends on "scientific and theological orthogenesis for which there is no evidence."[71] This conclusion can be applied with equal force to the general impetus to compress our scientific and theological understanding into an integrated whole through the interpretive lens of process thought. It is highly questionable whether the integrity of the scriptural or scientific informer is able to survive this integrative effort in any tenable way. Moreover, it certainly fails to resolve the tension residing in the interstices of the science and theology dialogue.

This integrative approach is beset by other challenges ranging from how to accommodate the Christian experience of prayer,[72] to questioning the utility of retrofitting evolutionary history with a fragmented assortment of deified lures with nebulous specifications. Suffice it to say, there is ample evidence to dispute the success of such a comprehensive integrative approach, so far as the resolution of tension is concerned.

We suggest that any process of integration needs to be more cognizant of the dynamic motion that inhabits the hermeneutical dimension. Strong integrative policies run the risk of inducing a collapse of the interpretive space where the scientific and theological spheres interact. This collapse is precipitated by the coalescence of our scientific and theological knowledge with restrictive principles of integrative governance like process thought. Integration as an ideal is then transformed into a totalizing objective that strongly orchestrates the communicative traffic from and between the scientific and scriptural informers. When this is the

---

71 M. A. Jeeves & R. J. Berry, *Science, Life, and Christian Belief: A Survey of Contemporary Issues*, Grand Rapids: Baker Books, 1998, 220.

72 Polkinghorne, *Faith, Science & Understanding*, New Haven: Yale University Press, 2000, 152.

case, it then becomes possible to declare that the integrative ideal has achieved the status of a metanarrative, which opens it to a similar Lyotardian critique that was employed earlier. Our orientation, in contrast, on the hermeneutical register, is to promote a greater degree of independence for each informer in order to circumvent the drift into an unwarranted restriction of the scope of an interpretive motion that garners insights from both informers.

The other end of the spectrum of *tension resolvers* is well represented by a theoretical model like complementarity, which emphasizes the distinctiveness of the scientific and theological realms. This perspective views science and theology as contending with the same subject but within different categories of description and explanation.[73] Employing the simple analogy of an electrical signboard and its different levels of description, Donald Mackay states, "once you understand the language of each description, what is there to be described in each is a matter of fact."[74] When this type of theoretical construct is applied to the engagement of science and theology, the result is a general reduction in the rivalry between them by a strategy that is dependent on a high degree of non-interference. In other words, tension tends to be eliminated by a type of "descriptive indexing." This all seems vaguely reminiscent of the modernist overtones that were discussed in the previous sections. In fact, Mackay at a later point states that scientists in formulating their descriptions should operate from a "detached spectator's standpoint."[75]

Categorical complementarity frequently borders on compartmentalization, particularly when it is strengthened with an overt

73 P. Duce, "Complementarity in Perspective," *Perspectives on Science and Christian Faith*, 8 (1996), 145-146.

74 D. M. Mackay, *The Clockwork Image: A Christian Perspective on Science*, Downers Grove: Intervarsity Press, 1974, 36-38.

75 Ibid., 38.

distinction between how and why questions.[76] In response to the accusation that science and theology offer non-interactive complementary perspectives, Richard Bube notes that these perspectives must be integrated to provide a coherent view of reality, but he does little more than to point to a statement of necessity. More attention is devoted to the separateness and partial nature of scientific and theological insights than to their integration.[77] How the scientific and scriptural descriptions engage in wider reflective considerations, other than simply being identified and presented, is left unclear.

Fraser Watts offers a less polarized complementary approach which downplays the radical differences between science and theology that unduly inhibit contact between them. He does, however, contend that as two discourses they are radically different, and that this point needs to be more strongly factored into the discussion by those promoting some form of dialogue between science and theology. Concerning religious language, for instance, Watts states, it "is broader in its scope and reference than scientific language, being personal and moral as well as making claims about the nature of reality."[78] However, he does leave a space for interaction when he discusses that the scientific and theological discourses are not independent unconnected discourses.[79]

In Lyotardian fashion, the recognition of the heterogeneity of discourses is a helpful contribution to the dismissal of authorita-

---

76 Duce in, *Reading the mind of God: Interpretation in Science and Theology*, Leicester: Apollos, 1998, 65-67 notes this in H. J. Van Till's strict separation between Scripture informing us about the relationship of the cosmos to God in "the categories of status, origin, governance, value and purpose" and science informing us about internal intelligibility in "the categories of physical properties, behavior and history." See H. J. Van Till, *The Fourth Day*, Grand Rapids: Eerdmans, 1986. Duce, for example, questions whether there is a clear distinction between governance and behavior. In particular, he asks which one does the formative history of life fall under?

77 R. H. Bube, *Putting It All Together: Seven Patterns for Relating Science and the Christian Faith*, Lanham: University Press of America, 1995, 167-172.

78 Watts, "Science and Theology as Complementary Perspectives," in *Rethinking Theology and Science: Six Models for the Current Dialogue*, Gregersen & van Huyssteen, eds., Grand Rapids: Eerdmans, 1998, 158-159. See also, Laughery, "Language at the Frontiers of Language," in *After Pentecost: Language and Biblical Interpretation*, C. Bartholomew, C. Greene, K. Möller, eds., Grand Rapids/Carlisle: Zondervan/Paternoster, 2001, 171-194, for a fuller discussion of religious and scientific language.

79 Ibid., 161-164.

tive declarations that consolidate all knowledge into a metanarrative, but the contrast between discourses can be exaggerated and fail to adequately contend with the interpretive workings in both scientific and nonscientific knowledge.[80] This seems to be the case with complementary models that promote a strong line of demarcation between scientific and theological discourses, so that the deposition of complementary statements becomes equated with interpretive resolution. Consequently, the evaluative projection of scientific or religious thought and discourse across domains of knowledge and into a broader realm of reflection is unduly attenuated by this approach.

The lack of containment of scientific and theological thought within well-defined parameters of discourse is particularly evident in the fields of evolutionary biology and sociobiology. Studies in these more synthetic areas break any sharply defined language barrier as they routinely contend with ethical and moral issues. Although he does not refer to it as such, from our general perspective, Stephen Gould supported a sort of secularized version of complementarity. However, when his evolutionary theorizing encountered concepts like progress and purpose within the contours of evolutionary biology, his scientific discourse became riddled with theological overtones that intersected his scientific ruminations to form a narrative-like description of the world.[81] The imposition of sharp divisions in language at these points would seem like a restrictive contrivance that too narrowly delim-

---

80 C. O. Schrag in *The Resources of Rationality*, Bloomington: Indiana University Press, 1992, 97-102, contends that what is lacking in Lyotard's thinking is adequate "recognition of the interpretive moment within both of the alleged forms of knowledge, 'narrative' and 'scientific' alike." Interpretation is at work regardless of the language game. For example, it is already at work before science even gets started by the delimitation of its discourse. In our discussion, this steers us away from over-structuring differences between scientific and theological (narrative) discourse.

81 S. J. Gould, *Ever Since Darwin: Reflections in Natural History*, New York: W. W. Norton, 1977, 12-13, notes that the Darwinian view of life has radical philosophical implications that challenge our entrenched Western sensibilities and replaces the traditional story of life with a new narrative that dismisses humanity as "the loftiest product of a preordained process." Thus, this type of scientific conclusion destabilizes the border between "scientific" and "narrative" (theological) thought and discourse.

its the inclusive nature of these interpretive moments.[82] Hence, scientists and nonscientists alike are not only interpreters, but are also storytellers as they allow interpretive and narrative elements to mix in an orthogonal trajectory across the "the various culture-spheres of" their "wider historical existence."[83]

It is undeniable that there is a place for complementary discourses, such as in the mind versus brain discussion, but we would contend that a format of partitioning is not immediately explanatory in function. John Polkinghorne concludes this when he states: "Complementarity is not an instantly explanatory concept. It is simply suggestive of a search for understanding which seeks to take an even-handed view of two accounts of what is going on."[84] This is reinforced by Nicholas Saunders' comments on divine action when he notes, "it is not the case that scientific and theological accounts of God's action are in some straightforward way complementary accounts of the same reality."[85] Furthermore, the determination of when these accounts are complementary or contradictory defies any simple formulations. Watts in concluding his remarks in a recent paper on the virtue of complementary perspectives notes the elusive nature of identifying any well-defined criteria for this kind of determination.[86] From our perspective, this deficiency should be viewed as indicative of the multifaceted unkempt nature and the contextually situated aspects of our hermeneutical endeavors.

---

82 Laughery, "Language at the Frontiers of Language," in *After Pentecost: Language and Biblical Interpretation*, 171-194, for a discussion of theological realism and language as creational.

83 Although Schrag in *The Resources of Rationality*, does not apply the concept that the consequences of interpretation and narrational emplotment are orthogonal to the culture-spheres directly to the science/theology discussion, we suggest that such an application is a helpful direction to pursue. It provides a necessary antidote to the overemphasis on contrast between the scientific and theological realms.

84 Polkinghorne, *Reason and Reality*, 27.

85 Saunders, *Divine Action & Modern Science*, 33.

86 Watts, "Science and Theology as Complementary Perspectives," 178.

Although we can appreciate the removal of strong either/or distinctions between scientific and theological perspectives, complementary approaches falter as a comprehensive interpretive program. In our judgment, by categorically harnessing the communicative resources of the scientific and scriptural informers, both a postmodern critique of modernism and substantial hermeneutical considerations are underplayed. Hence, as a comprehensive program that places analysis and classification in a decisive role, it tends to exchange the tensions of interpretive grappling in our quest for intelligibility and understanding for a type of structuralism tainted with modernist residue.

Conclusion

We certainly recognize that all of the positions discussed in addition to the relevant issues raised deserve far greater elaboration. However, our objective in this cursory scan of some of the ways science and theology interact was simply to draw out two significant points. First, whatever scheme is employed to contend with this interaction must give strong credence to the hermeneutical contours implicit in the engagement. As pointed out earlier, hermeneutics is at the core of our understanding and this necessitates the recognition of a hermeneutical realism in the discussion that draws from the quarters of postmodern analysis and defies any strict definitional parameters. And secondly, the residue from acknowledging this ontology includes the recognition that a persistent tension is present within our interpretive motion that eludes total resolution. This tension has existed historically in these discussions and continues to this day. In combination, these factors drive us to the conclusion that this tension is ontological in nature and at best can be minimized but not eliminated. In this sense, configurations that engulf the scientific and theological perspectives and evoke an absolute sense of certainty or domination represent illusionary symbols of interpretive resolution as they fall within the gravitational pull of metanarrative tendencies.

We would suggest that in light of these considerations, a more dynamic trajectory for a science and theology interaction may be found in expanding Kai Nielsen's concept of a wide reflective equilibrium[87] in a manner that recognizes a four part symphonic orchestration of being, knowledge, distinction and relatedness.[88] As pointed out by Calvin Schrag, reflection in this concept is viewed as "from bottom up social, always situated within the density of world-engagements." Schrag goes on to note that the dynamics of this reflection consists of a transversal back and forth movement across culture-spheres in a manner that effects a type of binding, "whereby each functions as a background for the other." In this reflective relationship there is due recognition of the distinctiveness of each sphere, but also acknowledgement of the propensity of each to provoke adjustments in the other.[89]

Van Huyssteen applies this concept directly to the science and theology discussion. He develops the notion of a postfoundationalist rationality, which is neither strictly modernist nor postmodernist in form, that strives for optimal understanding by encompassing our scientific and theological reasoning strategies within a "process of intercontextual and cross-disciplinary reflection."[90] If viewed as a relationship situated in the transversal time-space of their respective communicative practices, the interface of our scientific and theological reflections is characterized by the "interplay of dissent and consent" that effects appropriate revisions or concurrence in optimizing our wider interpretive understand-

---

87 K. Nielsen, "Searching for an Emancipatory Perspective: Wide Reflective Equilibrium and the Hermeneutical Circle," in *Anti-Foundationalism and Practical Reasoning*, E. Simpson, ed., Edmonton, AB: Academic Press, 1987,148-149.

88 See Laughery, *Living Hermeneutics in Motion*, 105-148, for an elucidation of how relation and distinction apply to the broader discussion of narrative and hermeneutics.

89 Schrag, *The Resources of Rationality*, 177-178.

90 van Huyssteen, *The Shaping of Rationality*, 278.

ing.[91] By discerning this transversal pattern of interpretation within a space of communicative praxis, we can hopefully avoid the slippage of a hermeneutical trajectory into the perils of another type of metanarrative.[92]

This brings us back to our designation of science and Scripture as informers. The term *informers* tried to capture their *relatedness* as complex communicative practices and their *distinctness* as designated and articulated by the spatio-temporal context of their respective practicing communities. The ecology of their interaction is not that of a predator-prey relationship or one of isolation, but more of a symbiotic community interwoven with a texture of creative tension that facilitates constructive critique, affirmation, conflict at times, and the forging of new perspectives. At the same time, this type of community weakens any hyper unifying attempts to dominate the interpretive landscape. As a result, among our epistemic values, humility must rank high in that as our convergent interpretive workings encounter the otherness of each informer it is imperative to be open to a continuous reassessment of our complex narratives of the world and the life we find in it. Thus, strong prescriptive remedies are destabilized as hermeneutically insensitive myths. Further elaboration of this type of communitarian symbiosis must await a future publication.

As we return to our starting point with Bernard Ramm, how do we respond to Ramm's assertion that there is no conflict between *true* science and Scripture? We shall answer in both the affirmative and the negative. We can concur that there is much that would support the ongoing interaction between science and Scripture as it pertains to the interpretation of the world and the life we find in it, despite claims to the contrary. However, there is also ample evidence to indicate that the tension between them

---

91 Schrag in *The Resources of Rationality*, 174, applies these concepts more generally, but we are focusing his thinking on the science and theology discussion.

92 Ibid., 76, 100-102.

continues to defy eradication, and in fact, often seems to have intensified. Therefore, the future of this dialogue must consider giving strong assent to this persistent tension as a permanent resident and inherent component of their ongoing intercourse.

INTERPRETING

SCIENCE AND SCRIPTURE

GENESIS 1-3

What is Life?

Resembles Life what once was held of Light,
Too ample in itself for human sight?
An absolute Self—an element ungrounded
All, that we see, all colours of all shade
By encroach of darkness made?
Is very life by consciousness unbounded?
And all the thoughts, pains, joys of mortal breath,
A war-embrace of wrestling Life and Death?[1]

These words, penned in the nineteenth century by the famous poet and author Samuel Taylor Coleridge, poetically capture the human quest to understand and explain life. Reflecting on this passage raises a host of questions. What is life, how do we perceive it, what does it mean, and what is the nature and charac-

---

1 S. T. Coleridge, *What is Life?* This poem is believed to have been written around 1805 and only published later in 1829.

ter of the world around us? Prior to the nineteenth century there was widespread agreement in the West, particularly in Protestant Christian circles, that resolution to these questions could be achieved by combining insights from both science and Scripture in a unified field of knowledge. If such an integrated view on the level of method and reference was established, it would become the focal point on which the understanding of life depended. Consequently, science and the Christian faith were presumed to be on the same side, mutually compatible, and dealing with the discovery of truth through a uniform epistemology. Today, many scholars find this approach untenable and aim to keep the two portrayals of life entirely separate.

In our eyes, one of the key problems in the science and Scripture discussion is that it is frequently characterized by a rigid double polarization. This polarization is often expressed as either a complete *distinction* that barricades exchange between them, or a comprehensive synthesis that collapses them together to create a tight and seamless *relation*. The hallmark of these approaches, represented in a variety of forms, is that the complexity of non-resolution is avoided at all cost. One of the major drawbacks of such double polarizations is the diminishment of tension, which in our judgment should remain rooted in the vital configuration of the relation *and* distinction between these two informers.

We highlighted, in the previous chapter, our view that both science and Scripture are informers that contribute to the interpretation of life.[2] In their role as informers, we began to make a case for a more candid dialogue between the two. We maintained that as we live in and work with the natural world and the biblical text, it is crucial to acknowledge that world and text are informers and therefore hermeneutical factors that have to contend with each other's stories. This challenging formulation, we argued,

---

2 See chapter 1.

shatters any notion of a reductionistic monologue that embraces one voice at the cost of the other, and suggests that a dynamic dialogical interaction is the way forward, allowing each informer to have a fecund role in a configuration of beginnings.

What are we to make of Scripture's contribution, in particular its Genesis 1-3 recounting, to the explanation and understanding of the world around us? Does science have a legitimate claim in conceiving itself to be an all encompassing story of beginnings in the face of and opposed to the early chapters of Genesis? Discussions in theological and scientific circles concerning these issues often occur without a clear sense of the general trajectory and orchestration of Genesis 1-3. There are some who engage with these chapters in a highly literalistic manner, while others ignore them completely. Our wager is that neither of these polarizations is an adequate orientation if we wish to have a better picture of our world. Paying close attention to the beats and rhythms of the text is essential for raising an awareness of its unfolding meaning and for challenging both literalist and disregarder.

Traditionally, there has been a diversity of approaches to Genesis 1-3. Form, source, historical, redaction and narrative criticism identify themselves either by seeking ways behind the text, detecting its structure, being able to decode and delimit its parts and pieces, or working with the unity or whole of the text. The revelatory, literary, theological, and historical context of Genesis 1-3 clearly fits into the whole of the Genesis narrative, the Pentateuch, and the megastory of the Scriptures. Although this narrative network opens up a myriad of directions that could be explored, our interest is in the more specific concern of how Genesis 1-3 is still able to speak into our scientifically informed, technologically advanced culture. We contend that a stronger articulation of the overall character, function, and genre of these chapters will contribute to our assessment of how the text can inform our ability to comprehend the natural world today.

Our aim in this chapter is to briefly explore three vital issues that, taken together, can point us toward a general configuration that best represents Genesis 1-3 in the science and Scripture discussion. These include the contextual setting of the story of creation, its narrative beginnings as a creation story; and finally, its narrative trajectories. Drawing from the concerted force of these investigations, we will then propose what we think is the most hermeneutically sound approach to the textual material. In conclusion, we will offer a provisional suggestion as to how Genesis 1-3 speaks as a valid and credible informer in our current context.

Interpretive Signals

Hermeneutical studies have emphasized the important role context should play in our interpretive strategies. In deciphering a text, what is being communicated and how it is being communicated is strongly shaped by the intellectual and literary environment of a particular historical, cultural, and linguistic context. This implies that the originating context, within which a text was composed, will be a limiting factor in determining how far we can stretch the text to speak into our context. In other words, recognition of context can give off interpretive signals that direct our thinking about how to configure and appropriate the text.

The early chapters of Genesis were framed within the literary conventions and conceptual world of the ancient Near East. A glimpse into this world can be gained by examining the literature and artifacts of the ancient Egyptian, Mesopotamian, and Canaanite cultures. Although there were cultural differences, we intend to minimize these and synthesize a general picture of what the encounter with the world was like in this environment.[3]

---

3   J. H. Walton, *Ancient Israelite Literature in its Cultural Context: A Survey of Parallels between Biblical and Ancient Near Eastern Texts*, Grand Rapids: Zondervan, 1990, 32.

When it came to nature, Conrad Hyers notes, "For most peoples in the ancient world, all the various regions of nature were divine."[4] Thus, natural phenomena were interpreted as and associated with the activities of an assortment of gods. Nature became endowed and saturated with the powers of deities. What was material, the sky or the sea for example, was personalized into the spiritual or ideal.[5] This personalization and deification of the natural world often carried over into the animal kingdom. Animals could function as representatives or forms of various divine beings.[6] The result of this blending of nature and religion is that explanations about how the natural world worked became embedded in a mythological dimension. Ancient Egyptians, for example, connected the alterations in the seasonal elevations of the sun and the ripening and rotting of crops with the power of heaven, the sky god.[7] Since the encounter with nature was intensely personal, the observation of nature and its orderly rhythms was aligned with human life through religious ritual and ceremony. Not surprisingly, early astronomers were also priests since the observation of the heavens was primarily a religious exercise.[8]

It seems safe to conclude that in this ancient context, conceptual partitions between natural and divine causation would have been difficult to comprehend. Consequently, this ancient "cognitive environment"[9] did not lend itself to either purely material explanations about the natural world or to the empirical exploration of that world. Thus, any correlation between our scientific

---

4 Hyers, *The Meaning of Creation: Genesis and Modern Science*, 44.

5 Alioto, *A History of Western Science*, 6.

6 For example: the bull-god Baal, the falcon-god Horus, the golden calf, etc. This divination could extend into the human realm as pharaohs, kings, and heroes were depicted as sons of god or mediators between the divine and human realm. See Hyers, 44.

7 Alioto, 8.

8 Ibid. 8.

9 We borrowed this term from Walton, *Ancient Near Eastern Thought and the Old Testament: Introducing the Conceptual World of the Old Testament*, Grand Rapids: Baker Academic, 2006, 21.

understanding and this ancient understanding of the world must be viewed cautiously. The common experience and description of the appearance of things should not be mistaken for an accurate statement as to their material properties and causes. The natural phenomena that these ancient people experienced were the same ones we experience, but how they were encountered and described was different in these ancient cultures.

Differences between the ancient context and ours can also be detected when we examine the ontological dimension. In the ancient Near East, something came into existence when it was separated out, named, and given a function.[10] The act of separation was associated with the process of creation and the establishment of order. The use of the separation motif is evident in both the ancient creation myths and the biblical text. The issuance of a name to an entity also had special significance in the ancient Near East, particularly in light of the deification of nature. It signified the entity's very essence and assigned a function or destiny to it.[11] For example, fifty names are conferred on Marduk in the *Enuma Elish* to declare his destiny and role as head of the gods.[12] This ancient ontological perspective stands in stark contrast to our scientific discussions about existence, which are dominated by more materialistic descriptions that focus on the physical properties of the world.

Another feature that plays prominently in the mythology of the ancient Near East is that the gods had origins. Not only was the world polytheistic, but there were family relationships between the gods. Separation and/or procreation were common procedures for the birth of the gods. The origin and existence of diverse gods would then be connected to their operational

---

10 Walton, *Ancient Near Eastern Thought*, 88.

11 Ibid. 188.

12 Ibid. 90.

roles in bringing about the natural phenomena in the world.[13] Explanations were hence overlaid with this mythical ordering of the world.

Frequently, the state of affairs before the creation of the cosmos is depicted as one that is unordered and uniform in character. These precosmic conditions were represented by water and darkness, which continued to lurk in the background of the created world in the form of the sea, dark night sky, and desert.[14] In this context, the creation of the cosmos involved bringing order and differentiation to the world out of this primordial state. In Mesopotamian mythology, the creation of the world included an element of conflict. The prime example of this can be found in the *Enuma Elish* where Marduk slays Tiamat and from her corpse the world is made. Tiamat's body is divided, again an act of separation, and boundaries are laid down for the waters to establish order. Sometimes, the pending forces of disorder were personalized. In Ugaritic myth, the chaotic forces could be represented in the form of the mythical sea monster Lothan or Leviathan, a seven-headed serpent that had to be overcome by the creator god to establish order.[15]

In summary, the composite perspective of the world in the ancient Near East was highly personalized, deified, and rooted in mythical stories and symbols of beginnings. Natural phenomena were described as they appeared and were explained within this mythical framework. In a nutshell this is the cultural milieu that forms the backdrop for Genesis' alternative story of beginnings.

What disruptive effect did this alternate story have? If we focus at the outset solely on the first creation story in Genesis

---

13 Van Till, *The Fourth Day*, 32-33.

14 Walton, *Ancient Near Eastern Thought*, 186.

15 B. W. Anderson, *Creation versus Chaos*, Philadelphia: Fortress, 1987, 134-135. However, R.A. Simkins in *Creator & Creation*, Peabody: Hendrickson, 1994, notes that "the conflict myth is a secondary development, a personification, of [the] primary creation metaphors of separation and differentiation." See p. 78.

1-2:4a, we can conclude that it deftly empties the natural world of meddling deities. In other words, it "clears the cosmic stage of its mythical scenes and polytheistic dramas, making way for different scenes and dramas, both monotheistic and naturalistic."[16] There is no theogony in this recounting. The Hebrew God stands alone as the Creator, without a beginning, related to and distinct from His creation. The story pictures one Divine Being who establishes creative authority over the entire natural order.

Thus, the Genesis creation story conceptually reorganizes the entire known world so that the cosmos and all that is in it are placed in creaturely status. For example, why are the sun and moon referred to as the greater and lesser light, respectively? There were certainly names in the Hebrew language to apply to these entities. Since the sun and moon were important deities in the ancient Near Eastern setting, this non-naming of them in Genesis seems to be a strategic move to forcefully remove them as deities in the world. From a functional point of view, the sun and the moon are to serve human existence not vice versa, suggesting a contextual reversal of roles in Genesis. Even the formulation of reproducing after its kind emphasizes the natural flow and order of things. No living creatures are divine or will transform into deity. The cosmic order "is now defined as nature."[17]

This first strike creation story is polemical in nature in that it uses the thought forms and symbols common to the ancient Near East and fills them with radically new meaning. Common literary and conceptual conventions like separation, differentiation, precosmic conditions,[18] and possibly allusions to chaos beasts[19]

---

16 Hyers, 47.

17 Ibid., 47.

18 Echoes from the ancient Near East context may be heard in Genesis 1:2 and 2:5 where water & darkness and desert-like conditions, respectively, may recall common conceptualizations of precosmic conditions.

19 On the fifth day of creation (verse 21), sea monsters are singled out for special treatment. The verb *bara*, reserved exclusively for God's creative action, is applied and may

are deployed in a well orchestrated and structured assault on the deification of nature with the result that the true Creator is identified. For example, the first three days of creation consist of strong acts of separation setting the boundaries of the cosmos in place so that it can be filled with diverse occupants. The world offers no resistance to the authority of the true Creator. One might even infer that the separation motif was extended into the third chapter where the Creator exits the scene and is thereby separated from the act of disobedience. With this twist in the story line, the identity and character of the Creator, as well as humanity's relationship with Him, is further exposed. Many other examples of conceptual correspondence between the biblical text and its cultural setting can be found.[20]

Nowhere is this correspondence more germane than when the subject of human origins is broached. Again, there are both parallels and differences between the biblical story of human origins and those from other contiguous cultures. Suffice it to say, however, the biblical description of human beginnings shares a degree of concordism with its cultural setting.[21]

It is important to note that there is no indication that the biblical text breaks with the cosmic geography of its time. The biblical reconfiguration of the world offered by the Genesis story of beginnings did not negate the prevailing notions of the structure of the world. There are ample Old Testament references that confirm the observation that the biblical authors deployed context-laden features of cosmic architecture in their understanding.[22]

hearken back to the importance of such creatures in Mesopotamian myth. The existence of such creatures is not negated, but simply placed under the creative authority of God. No conflict here, just submission. See E. Lucas, *Interpreting Genesis in the 21ˢᵗ Century*, published by the Faraday Institute for Science and Religion, April 2007.

20 See Simkins, *Creator & Creation*, and Walton, *Ancient Near Eastern Thought.*

21 The ancient Near Eastern setting encourages the view that Adam and Eve be understood in archetypal terms. See Walton, *Ancient Near Eastern Thought,* 208-209.

22 There is good reason to believe that the 3-tiered cosmic architecture of the ancient Near East was presupposed by the ancient Hebrews. Basically, the architecture consisted of a flat,

Furthermore, there is no sign that the story of beginnings in Genesis led to any immediate paradigm breaking-thoughts about the architecture of the cosmos. What is altered by the Genesis story is not new thinking about the structure and form of the natural world; but rather, the theological perspective of the world. The natural world, no matter what form it took, was structurally decoupled from its Creator and "naturalized" as a creation. Accordingly, humanity's role was freed from the false religious service to the deified components of the world.

The inevitable conclusion is that the delivery system of the biblical informer is packaged with the conceptual and literary features of its context. As we have seen, in many ways the early chapters of Genesis share a common understanding about the architectural features of the world that were widely held at the time; while in other ways, they offer a radically unique theological interpretation that explains the origin and existence of the natural world in a revolutionary manner. Therefore, the configuration and interpretation of the early chapters of Genesis is strongly influenced by, yet not reduced to, its ancient Near East context.

Interpreting Beginnings

In the beginning there was God: then came humans, hermeneutics, narrative, and later, Genesis 1-3. As we have highlighted in the previous section, these chapters portray God as the unrivaled Creator who has authority over the world and humanity. The God of the Hebrews is declared to be the God of the story of beginnings. Early Genesis then is scripted from the ancient Hebrew perspective that God had revealed Himself in and acted through text, nature, and nation to make Himself known.

. . . .

disk-like earth floating on water that was supported by pillars with the heavens above and the netherworld beneath. The dome-like sky, which the sun and stars tracked through, was relatively solid and held back the cosmic waters. References to the features of this cosmic structure can be found in a number of biblical references. See, for example, Genesis 1:20, Job 9:6-7, Job 22:14, Psalm 24:2, Psalm 104: 2-3, Isaiah 40:22.

Several notions of hermeneutics permeate the landscape of the science and theology discussion today.[23] Our position is that hermeneutics, at the outset of the revealing Genesis narrative, plays a key role as the biblical writer offers a reflective interpretation of the world and God. That is, interpretation is neither fault nor detriment, but has been present from the beginning of creation.[24] Being hermeneutical then is partially constitutive of what it means to be human, whether biblical author or contemporary *"reader"* of the text and/or world. The force of this ontological reality highlights our finitude and translates into the recognition that all, including both biblical interpreters and scientists, are "situated" interpreters that operate from within context-laden environments. This negates any pretense of naïve idealism or neutral realism.

Consequently, the lens through which we are configuring this chapter is that of being hermeneutical realists. There are at least two points that emerge from this acknowledgment. First, as realists we believe that a world exists that can be known, and our knowledge of the world informs our interpretation of reality. Therefore, the world is far more than a mere projection or construction of our mind. Second, being hermeneutical means that we are always pre-involved interpreters of the world. Interpretation initially unfolds from inside a gender, place, time, culture, and so forth, not outside it. This interpretive reality encompasses who we are as knowers and needs to be plainly in view in contending with scientific, theological, or any other issues.

While in our contemporary context hermeneutics is deeply connected to human understanding, one of its previous considerations and no doubt an equally valid concern today is the interpretation of texts, particularly biblical texts.[25] As we approach

---

23 See chapter 1.

24 J. K. A. Smith, *The Fall of Interpretation: Philosophical Foundations for a Creational Hermeneutic*, Downers Grove: IVP, 2000.

25 See chapter 1, esp. 2-6.

Genesis 1-3, it is important to recognize that, hermeneutically speaking, biblical texts have the capacity to inform and shape our understanding and explanation of God, ourselves and the world leading to new understanding.[26] More specifically, biblical stories reveal God and open up new ways of seeing, knowing, and being in the world, which is vital to the hermeneutical enterprise. This trajectory implies that we are not left alone to be our own referents, and that the epistemological horizon of the biblical text cannot be ignored when it comes to a proper consideration of hermeneutics.

Building on the previous paragraphs, we suggest that a detour through the Genesis 1-3 world will provide us with three significant vectors that are hermeneutically relevant. First, we have a text that still vies for a place in our general interpretation of the world. Second, the text informs and expands our ontological understanding as being is "called out" and spoken to from beyond the realms of self indulgence, entrapment, or containment. Third, there is an action-oriented, unfolding representation of the natural world presented in the text.

Having clarified our hermeneutical stance, we now turn to focus more closely on Genesis 1-3. Genesis, as story, functions at a number of levels and our task is to listen to the text and its orchestration. How do we hear the text? First, Genesis 1-3 is *revelatory*. As noted in the previous section, the story gives readers a unique Godly revelation referenced portrait of beginnings, related to but distinct from other ancient Near Eastern perspectives. This is not a present day story, yet the text maintains the capacity to speak from its own time into ours. Second, Genesis 1-3 is a *historical* text. The term historical is not to be understood as referring to a detailed and precise account of beginnings, but rather as a mega-recounting using bold and broad brush strokes, thereby leaving behind a substantial number of unresolved questions. Third, Genesis 1-3 is *literature*. Written as narrative, it is a literary act

26 Ibid., 6-16.

laced with drama and saturated with symbolic artistry that engages the imagination of the reader. And finally, Genesis 1-3 is a *theological* text. That is, it informs readers about God and the truth that Israel's God created nature and humanity.

Thus, these early chapters of Genesis combine the revelatory, historical, literary, and theological levels of orchestration into an interwoven organic whole that creates a polyphonic recounting of beginnings. To take the musical analogy further, listening to Genesis 1-3 is like hearing a symphony perform wherein a number of different instruments, rhythms, and notes coalesce to produce an emerging sound offered to interpretation.

While there may be general agreement as to what parts make up the total orchestration of the text as traced out in the previous paragraphs, debates and polarizations often flare up over which part best defines these chapters. This leads to a tendency to interpret Genesis 1-3 solely and conclusively in terms of its revelatory, historical, literary, or theological dimension, and thereby loses the overall polyphonic discourse of the text. Returning to our musical analogy, this is like listening to a solo instrument playing when the score calls for the concerted action of the whole orchestra. To finally single out one part of the score at the exclusion of others results in a divide and conquer type of hermeneutical strategy that has more in common with a modernist critical paradigm than it does with the configuration of an ancient text.[27]

Attentive to this ancient backdrop for Genesis 1-3 and in full view of the symphonic orchestration of the text that consists of revelatory,

---

27 We would agree with the assessment of many authors who note that early Genesis is not a scientific text and that context-dependent theological issues are of utmost importance to the text's communicative purposes. See Lucas, "Science and the Bible: Are They Incompatible?" *Science and Christian Belief* 17 (2005), 137-154 and *Interpreting Genesis*. However, we would argue that the proper contrast is not between a theological text and a scientific one, but between a scientific text and an ancient one that is imaginatively and poetically formatted within the framework of the Hebrews existence and their attending knowledge of God and the world. On this register, the early chapters of Genesis would function as more than merely a theological or historical text inasmuch as they are expressly connected to the larger meganarrative picture of God's unfolding interaction with humanity in general, and Israel in particular.

literary, theological, and historical rhythms, we readily acknowledge that there is a *provisional* place for drawing out and listening to each rhythmic part of the text. However, each part must eventually be reinserted into a tensional web of the interactive whole where it contributes to the overall function and configuration of Genesis 1-3, and where each part's meaning and purpose is more fully discovered. With this caveat in mind, we intend to momentarily break the historical part out for closer inspection since it has been a source of considerable controversy.[28] Furthermore, by identifying the kind of historical rhythms that play through the text, we will be in a better position to determine what general configuration best suits Genesis 1-3. But again, these historical rhythms must ultimately re-connect into the harmonics of the whole textual orchestration in a compatible way. Later, we will pursue the task of re-connection, but for now, what does it mean to call Genesis 1-3 historical?

Discussions concerning the truth value of history have had a long tradition and more recently postmodern ideas have broken onto the scene, creating and arguing for new ways of viewing history and historiography.[29] Disagreements flourish on this issue: however, we shall not respond here to the wide diversity of views represented.[30] Rather, we wish to briefly address an important, though frequently neglected question which arises on this register and applies to all disciplines, especially biblical interpretation:[31] What is history? An answer may appear obvious, until someone asks us to clarify and elucidate.

---

28 No doubt any of the four rhythms could be explored and listened to more carefully.

29 K. Jenkins, *Re-Thinking History*, London: Routledge, 1991; *The Postmodern History Reader*, ed., London: Routledge, 1997. A. Munslow, *Deconstructing History*, London: Routledge, 1997. P. Zagorin, "History, the Referent, and Narrative Reflections on Postmodernism Now," *History and Theory* 38, (1999), 1-24.

30 Laughery, "Ricoeur on History, Fiction and Biblical Hermeneutics," in: *'Behind' the Text: History and Biblical Interpretation*, C. Bartholemew, C. S. Evans, M. Healy, M. Rae, eds., Grand Rapids/Carlisle: Zondervan/Paternoster, 2003, 339-362.

31 B. Halpern, *The First Historians: The Hebrew Bible and History*, University Park: Pennsylvania State University Press, 1996.

Elaboration of the historical rhythm of the text can be aided by considering the relation and distinction between history and historiography. The word history, from our perspective, has the capacity to refer to actual past events in time, while historiography is defined as the complex matter of interpreting and recounting a selection of these events thematically and configuring them into a written narrative.[32] Consequently, event and textual representation of the past never have a one to one correspondence, yet this does not undermine the capacity of historiography to have historical credibility. Based on these distinctions, the wide-ranging genre of Genesis 1-3 can be identified as historiography. But, if the first three chapters of Genesis carry a historical rhythm, how should we configure this part of the text in a manner that keeps it tuned into its context, yet does not reduce it to merely its context?

Paul Ricoeur has given us an interesting perspective that may contribute to this controversial aporia.[33] According to Ricoeur, the philosophy of history has moved away from the grand schemes of Hegel or Marx and their notions of universal history to more modest aims of reflecting on the work and critical engagement of the historian. One of the advantages of this trajectory is that the historian is understood to be situated in, as opposed to being viewed as located outside the work of writing history.

Ricoeur maintains that there are three types of historiography, or written interpretive accounts of events in time, and each

---

32 Following P. R. Davies and J. Rogerson, *The Old Testament World*, Englewood Cliffs: Prentice Hall, 1989, 218. See also, Laughery, *Living Hermeneutics in Motion: An Analysis and Evaluation of Paul Ricoeur's Contribution to Biblical Hermeneutics*.

33 Ricoeur has been a formidable force in a diversity of discussions, including those related to interpreting Scripture and science. See "Sur l'exégèse de Genèse 1,1-2,4a," in: *Exégèse et herméneutique*, X. Leon Dufour, ed., Paris : Seuil, 1971, 57-97; *Philosophie de la volonté. Finitude et culpabilité II, La symbolique du mal*, Paris: Aubier, 1960 (*The Symbolism of Evil*); *Essays on Biblical Interpretaion*, L. S. Mudge, ed., Philadelphia: Fortress, 1980; *Ce qui nous fait penser? La nature et la règle*, avec Jean-Pierre Changeux, Paris: Odile Jacob, 2000 (*What Makes us Think? A Neuroscientist and A Philosopher Argue About Ethics, Human Nature and the Brain*, trans., M. B. DeBevoise, Princeton: Princeton University Press, 2002); *Penser la bible*, avec A. LaCocque, Paris: Seuil, 1998 (*Thinking Biblically*, trans., D. Pellauer, Chicago: University of Chicago Press, 1998.)

have a link to the other. In order to illustrate the point, we shall use the metaphor of a battle to distinguish different kinds of historical writing. First, the documentary type of historiography seeks to establish what battle was fought and won, by whom and when. Second, the explicative type aims to recount the results of the battle from a social, political, or economic angle. And third, the poetic type takes the reality of the past, interprets why the battle was won, and then shapes it into a narrative through which a community of readers understands itself in the present. One of the outstanding values of Ricoeur's taxonomy is that it alerts us to the possibility that there are several legitimate ways of writing history, not just one credible way.[34]

Returning to Genesis 1-3, we would argue that the text displays the more prominent features of a poetic historiography, while not completely excluding the cumulative character of the other historiographical aims. That is, the text incorporates a number of levels of historiography in order to reveal a larger portrait of God and life than a straight documentary historiography with its factual selectivity (although such selectivity is not entirely irrelevant to the informing nature of the text). The Genesis story, for example, is not centered on giving a list of empirically verifiable historical or scientific facts, but it actually interprets and redescribes the world from within and beyond the boundaries of space and time, naming Israel's God as the one and only God—the great Creator in the unfolding drama of beginnings. In this narrative portrayal God is powerfully at work, among other things, creating, speaking, commenting, blessing, and providing. The genius of Genesis 1-3 rests in its magnificent panoply of operative layers of contentful subversive convergence, interconnected on the register of

---

34 Ricoeur, "Philosophies critiques de l'histoire: Recherche, explication, écriture," in: *Philosophical problems today*, G. Fløistad, ed., vol 1, Dordrecht : Kluwer, 1994, 139-201. D. Marguerat, *Le première histoire du christianisme*, Paris: Cerf, 1999, (*The First Christian Historian*, trans., Laughery, K. McKinney, R. Bauckham, Cambridge: Cambridge University Press, 2002, 5-25).

imagination (writer and reader), but disconnected at the level of revelatory reference (God). Thus, the chapters reveal, convey, and represent a selection of God actions and sayings, various occurrences, people, situations and contexts that have left traces in the world which evoke the reality of the past and interpret it so that God's people will have an explanation and new understanding of something of who the creator God is, who they are, and what the natural world is like.

The historiography of Genesis 1-3 on this register is a cumulative poetic historiography and a meeting place for the relation and distinction between imaginative literary art and thematic eventful interpretive recounting. In this case, recounting imaginatively in symbolic formulations is not the same thing as imaginary recounting.[35] The former refers to creative artistry in interpreting and vividly representing an understanding of God and the world in a manner connected to its time, while the latter concerns escape and fantasy that becomes a referent for itself.[36] Biblical authors, as Sailhamer contends in an essay on Genesis, were attempting to connect their stories to the world that was really there. He puts it this way:

> By representing reality in their narratives, they were defining its essential characteristics. This is surely not to say they were making it up. There is every reason to maintain that the world we find depicted in these narratives was, in fact, intended by them to be identified as the real world.[37]

---

35 E. A. Speiser, "The Rivers of Paradise," in: J. J. Finkelstein and M. Greenberg, eds., *Oriental and Biblical Studies: Collected Writings of E. A. Speiser*, Philadelphia: University of Pennsylvania Press, 1967, 23-34.

36 A biblical worldview maintains that there is a real world which is related to and distinct from God and the cultural constructions and productions of science or theology. How could there be an imaginary if there was no real world from which to evaluate and measure? In other words, a necessary presupposition for the imaginary is the real, and it could not exist without it. On this register, imaginary is parasitic, as it must presuppose that which it is not in the attempt to have a theater of its own.

37 J. H. Sailhamer, *Introduction to Old Testament Theology*, Grand Rapids: Zondervan, 1995, 290.

As a cumulative poetic historiography, the early chapters of Genesis are not a straight-telling of history, but rather a skillfully recounted story of beginnings precipitated by the action's of the divine Creator and based on the Hebrews' encounter with the living God of Abraham, Isaac, and Jacob. This founding narrative, a poetic historiography, is attested to by the way God speaks, acts, engages, and intervenes in a symbolic scenario that recounts according to its goals and purposes that this God, as the God of Israel, is the only true God. The detection and recognition of the historiographical character and quality of the text heightens our awareness that forlorn attempts to interpret it in a reductionistic manner, by imposing contemporary standards of history writing, is unwarranted and superfluous. Exclusionary strategies act as a catalyst for historiographical confusion and fail to be attuned to the complex poetic filaments which make up the ancient Genesis narrative.[38]

Retaining and building on the Ricoeurian notion of poetic historiography, we would like to take this configuration a step further. Thus, we propose the notion that Genesis 1-3 is a *poetic* text and offer this as a constructive way forward for its interpretation. Poetic, in our eyes, is the act and art—a creative mimesis rolled into the verb poïesis—of making *saturated phenomena*.[39] By saturated phenomena, we mean that this story of beginnings is divinely-driven and imaginatively pre-loaded with a demonstration of God's creative action, guidance, and organization that results in meaningful layers of explanation and new understanding about God, humanity, and the world. This poetic rendition of the text allows it to function as a symbiotic community, where the different

---

38 For insights on biblical narrative see, M. Sternberg, *The Poetics of Biblical Narrative: Ideological Literature and the Drama of Reading*, Bloomington: Indiana University Press, 1985, 1987. R. Alter, *The Art of Biblical Narrative*, New York: Basic Books, 1981. V. P. Long, *The Art of Biblical History*, Grand Rapids: Zondervan, 1994.

39 See J-L. Marion, *Etant donné: Essai d'une phénoménologie de la donation*, Paris: Presses Universitaires de France, 1997. (*Being Given: Toward A Phenomenology of Giveness*, trans., J. L. Kosky, Stanford: Stanford University Press, 2002, 199-220, for somewhat similar terminology— saturated phenomenon, although with a different meaning).

downloads into the story perform a mutually enhancing, yet tensional dialogue. For example, whatever differences exist between the two biblical creation accounts may not merely reflect different traditions in the Hebrew community,[40] but may be part of a larger symbiosis as strands of relevant thought converge into an organic whole that is not unduly burdened by the need to rig the material for complete correspondence between the accounts.[41]

In summary, these early chapters in Genesis comprise a two-fold convergence. First, the revelatory, historical, theological, and literary rhythms that God is the Creator are configured and inseparably interlinked in this story of beginnings. While each of these rhythms can be explored and developed on their own, as we have done with the historical (and could have done with others), the text's trajectory cannot finally be reduced to any one of them. Second, operative levels of historiography are skillfully, artistically, and symbolically interwoven into a poetic recounting that God the Creator has acted in creating the world. Consequently, these chapters defy a *strip mining* approach so prevalent today which endeavors to merely embrace one of the parts.[42] The veins run too deep and are so intimately intertwined into an organic whole that any ultimate textual dissection which disregards this unity will underplay the provocative nature of the text. As Gudas points out:

> In contemporary criticism 'organic,' though widely used, has all but lost its metaphoric significance. The term is claimed by or attributed to critical systems which hold that the chief concern of criticism should be with the unity of the literary work. Thus it follows that

---

40 Hyers, 41.

41 Due to lack of space here, further elaboration of this perspective will have to await a future publication.

42 J. B. Doukhan, *The Genesis Creation Story: Its Literary Structure*, Berrien Springs: Andrews University Press, 1978, who refers to these early chapters of Genesis as a profound unity, characterized by a conscious literary act.

the parts of an artistic whole have qualities, meanings, or effects which they would not have separately and that the most important excellence that can be attributed to any of the parts is to show that it is a necessary element of that whole.[43]

In that there is no absolute object or subject, at least on the level of knowledge, an organic poetic configuration may rightly offer interpreters a greater flexibility when engaging text and world, and therefore counter various forms of reductionism. Hence, we suggest that Genesis 1-3 is a poetic text that re-describes reality in a story of beginnings, which deftly and artistically brings us into God's world.

While in one sense Genesis 1-3 is deeply embedded in its context and therefore should not be viewed as a precise scientific-like informer, in another sense it transcends and cannot be reduced to a scientific categorization.[44] For example, this text tells us nothing about DNA, cells, and molecules; yet, it has the capacity to capture an accurate, innovative, enduring, and always avant-garde portrayal of nature as a general category and place of contact between God, humanity, and other creatures.

Interpreting Trajectories

Today more than ever interpreters are drawing on the knowledge of histories, societies, cultures, natural sciences and texts to explain the world. A noteworthy feature of this orientation has been a rediscovery of the relevance of narrative. Dramatic fascination with stories and the worlds they create, represent, and signify has now become a prominent feature in the quest for the meaning of life in the late twentieth and early twenty-first centuries. This interest in narrative has clearly marked our times in a sur-

---

43 See *The Princeton Encyclopedia of Poetry and Poetics*, A. Preminger, ed., London: Macmillan, 1975, 593-594.

44 See chapter 1.

prising way. When it seemed as if the unquestionable merits of a mechanical, technological, and scientifically-driven world would have explained the entirety of life, stories have again released and captured the attention of imaginations, hearts, and minds. From this strong contemporary interest in narrative, a basic question arises: What is narrative? While a full answer to this question, which David Carr has identified as the battle ground for the disciplines,[45] lies beyond the scope of this chapter,[46] it is nevertheless important to highlight key elements in the discussion as they will apply to Genesis 1-3.

We again turn to the work of Ricoeur, who addressed the 'what is narrative' question in his three volume work *Temps et récit (Time and Narrative)*.[47] To be sure, narrative is a story with a narrator, plot, characters, action, time, intrigue, conflict, point of view, and mystery. Yet according to Ricoeur, narrative is not merely a traditional story of representation. Ricoeur's notion of narrative is that it creates a world—something new is created that did not previously exist. This narrative world is meant to be entered, inhabited, and appropriated by the reader. As the reader dwells in the created world of the story, new possibilities are opened up for articulating and conveying truth and meaning. Hence, on this understanding, narrative is a semantic innovation in that it configures a world that has the potential power to refigure the reader's world.

To take the discussion of narrative a step further, we turn to a brief description of Ricoeur's notion of a three-fold mimesis.[48]

---

45 D. Carr, "Ricoeur on Narrative," in: D. Wood, ed., *On Paul Ricoeur: Narrative and Interpretation*, London: Routledge, 1991, 160-187, esp. 160-173. Laughery, *Living Hermeneutics*, 113.

46 See Laughery, *Living Hermeneutics*, for a fuller treatment of this vital issue.

47 Ricoeur, *Temps et récit*, 3 tomes, Paris: Seuil, 1983-1985. (*Time and Narrative*, 3 vols, trans., K. McLaughlin and D. Pellauer, vols. 1-2; K. Blamey and D. Pellauer, vol. 3, Chicago: University of Chicago Press, 1984-1987).

48 Mimesis is a creative imitation of action—"the dynamic sense of making a representation, a transposition into representative works," resulting in the art of composition. See Ricoeur, *Time and Narrative*, vol. 1, 31-37.

Mimesis I operates as a *pre-figurative* capacity to detect action versus mere motion. Actions are connected to motives and goals, symbols, and time, and to the questions of "who" and "why." Mimesis II is a specific literary act that creates a world and *configures* actions into a structured timeframe of beginning, middle, and end. Mimesis III occurs when the reader's world is connected to the story world and through entering that world, taking possession of it, and being possessed by it, their own world is *refigured*.[49]

Emplotment is a key for understanding mimesis II. To *make* a plot, for Ricoeur, is a synthesis of the heterogeneous in the following ways. First, it makes one story out of a multiplicity of incidents. Second, plot organizes unintended circumstances, relationships between actors, and planned or unplanned encounters, drawing them together into a single story. And third, a plot provides a time totality in the story, which can be understood as a creative act of configuration out of a succession of events.[50] This Ricoeurian notion of plot making, coupled with the poetic historiography of Genesis 1-3, has the power to weld together interpreted actions and thematic events into an organic narrative whole.

Written from the vantage point of the sacred experience of God over many years, the Genesis story of beginnings opens up a new way for the Hebrew writer to testify to that which was already known in Israel.[51] God, nature, and humanity were not the "who" and the "why" that other ancient Near Eastern stories had configured them to be (Mimesis I & II). Thus, these early chapters of Genesis are a product of sedimentation and innovation culminating in a revealing narrative of God's story (Mimesis I & II). Like a transfusion, the life of God's people flows into this narrative recounting of beginnings, while in turn the story

---

49 Ibid., 52-87. Also see Laughery, *Living Hermeneutics*, 131-162, for a fuller discussion.

50 See Ricoeur, *Time and Narrative*, vol. 1, 38-50.

51 Doukhan, *Genesis*, 246, states: "Revelation implies Reality and both imply a real existential engagement with the One who revealed."

flows back out into the life of Israel, the prophets, the apostles and the churches, surging right through and having the capacity to powerfully refigure the lives of readers today and in the future (Mimesis III).

As we have observed in the previous paragraph, Genesis 1-3 presents an unfolding drama of creation. This story of beginnings, written for God's people, narrates a point of arrival where God, nature, and humanity appear, and it also marks a point of departure from which life can unfold. The saturated revelatory story of beginnings dynamically transforms and continually radicalizes our understanding of God, nature, and humanity and functions as a catalyst for all that follows in its wake. In our judgment, one of the chief aims of this creation semantic innovation is to draw the reader into God's "sacred world" of beginnings and to illuminate the path ahead for the people of God. Consequently, there is a significant forward moving trajectory in the narrative concerning the nature of the world, the relation and distinction of God to it, and the life of the people of God. Several examples can be highlighted: land, blessings, Sabbath, family, covenant, nation, sacrifice, and sanctuary-temple are noteworthy connecting filaments that electrify this early recounting of the times.[52] Therefore, in reading Genesis 1-3 readers' lives are refigured in line with the truth of the revelation of the Creator as they become part of the intricate web of connections that stream in, out, and ripple through the biblical story and its relation and distinction to the world. In this sense, the Genesis 1-3 narrative is a "living" text.

Narrative, Carr suggests, is a form of life before it is a form of discourse.[53] From this perspective, Genesis 1-3 represents a form

---

[52] G. J. Wenham, "Sanctuary Symbolism in the Garden of Eden Story," in: R. S. Hess and D. T. Tsumura, eds., *I Studied Inscriptions from Before the Flood: Ancient Near Eastern, Literary, and Linguistic Approaches to Genesis 1-11*, Winona Lake: Eisenbrauns, 1994, 399-404. Wenham helpfully focuses on the Eden portrait as "sanctuary symbolism." We believe the other filaments in the story are connected and can be developed in a similar fashion.

[53] Carr, "Ricoeur," 160-173.

of life that is translated into a story. While this story is a revelatory semantic innovation, it is prefigured by and configured from a lived life in the world. Consequently, the narrative point of view is made up of a constellation of complex interactions flowing from God, author, narrator, character, audience, and world, and then back through world, audience, character, narrator, author, and God. This spherical refraction alters, yet imaginatively represents reality by narrating it as a story of beginnings.

Conclusion

We began this chapter with the provocative words of Coleridge, who poetically probed the fascinating question: What is Life? Answers to this enigmatic mystery today, whether coming from Scriptural or scientific quarters, are understood to be complex and diverse. As we have seen, discussions on this topic are often marked by strong polarizations that tend to negate the contribution of either the scriptural or scientific informer.

In our view, this situation may be alleviated to some extent by reconsidering and identifying the proper configuration of the early chapters of Genesis. While it is clear that Genesis 1-3 lends itself to closer examination at several levels, our objective was to listen to the various rhythms of its orchestration, and to provisionally hear the controversial historical rhythm of the text, before re-integrating it into its symphonic whole.

Our critique of mutually exclusive hermeneutical strategies that in the final analysis atomize the text into revelatory, historical, literary, or theological hegemony (though each plays a part in the whole), brought us to the conclusion that the biblical story of beginnings can best be seen as a cumulative historiographical poetic narrative. Drawing from Ricoeur's helpful insights lends credence to the idea that the story of beginnings in Genesis is an imaginative and revelatory semantic innovation—a *founding narrative*, framed by Israel's illuminating encounter with the Creator and the world of the time. Thereby, this founding narrative is enabled to form links with the unfolding realities of Israel's unique identity and covenantal relationship with the God of Abraham, Isaac, and Jacob. Furthermore, the narrative trajectory functions in a historical sense as an identifiable location of God's arrival and as the point of departure for the whole biblical story. As a revelatory, historical, theological, and literary-oriented orchestration, it can be deployed as both reference and backdrop for God's continuing and future actions in the world.

So, where does Genesis 1-3's credibility lie for both science and Scripture? It lies in the "power of story" where imagination and the revelatory realities of God, and the world He created meet. The biblical story of beginnings brings together the meaningful structure of reality without wedding itself to a static architectural statement about the world. Through our engagement with God's story, our vision of the world is changed and placed within the same trajectory that the ancient Hebrews experienced. Consequently, these early chapters of Genesis are best understood as an organic poetic text that re-describes reality placing it in a sacred and destiny oriented context that invites the reader into a world—God's unfolding world. In this sense, the text is a living text that recycles our interpretive trajectory through a poetic network of divine and creaturely actions, purposes, and goals.

IN TIME

The Drama of a Narrative-Based Hermeneutical Approach to the Early Chapters of Genesis

Mutability

From low to high doth dissolution climb,
And sink from high to low, along a scale
Of awful notes, whose concord shall not fail;
A musical but melancholy chime,
Which they can hear who meddle not with crime,
Nor avarice, nor over-anxious care.
Truth fails not; but her outward forms that bear
The longest date do melt like frosty rime,
That in the morning whitened hill and plain
And is no more; drop like the tower sublime
Of yesterday, which royally did wear
His crown of weeds, but could not even sustain
Some casual shout that broke the silent air,
Or the unimaginable touch of Time.[1]

The perennial struggle to understand time and change have been the trade of many poets, philosophers, scientists, and theologians throughout the centuries. Our dilemma of living

---

1   W. Wordsworth, *Ecclesiastical Sketches,* 1822.

in time, aptly expressed above in William Wordsworth's poem, leads to the following types of questions: what is time and how does life in time concord with the steady hand of unfailing truth? Portrayed in this poetic rendition of the temporal side of life is the general sense that change is in the air, while so much seems to remain the same. The enigma of time is an important dimension of this chapter and we will return to it later, but first we would like to briefly set the stage for our exploration of the early Genesis creation story.

In our contemporary context, attempts to comprehend the world around us with its manifold features, like time, are frequently trapped in scientific evaluations.[2] Entrapment of this kind is not surprising when one considers that the explanatory equilibrium has shifted away from more traditional/religious sources toward giving a stronger role to the more empirically-based sciences. This change of direction has raised a cluster of questions and issues that can often leave non-scientific sources on the defensive. Consequently, earlier visions of the world, which were strongly or almost exclusively informed by other sources like the biblical text, have undergone considerable reassessment. In light of such re-evaluation, a piercing question that will be interwoven into the heart of our study emerges: what *informing* stature does the Genesis portrait of beginnings have today?

Centuries ago, notable figures like Copernicus, Kepler, and Galileo presented a new disruptive configuration of nature that opened the door wide for productive and corrective hermeneutical exchange between science and Scripture.[3] However, by opening this door, the biblical informer became inadvertently vulner-

---

2 S. Hawking in *A Brief History of Time: From the Big Bang to Black Holes*, London: Bantam Press, 1988, 145, denotes three arrows of time that give it directionality. These are the thermodynamic (increase in entropy), psychological, and cosmological (related to an expanding universe) arrows of time.

3 For further details see A. G. Debus, *Man and Nature in the Renaissance*, Cambridge: Cambridge University Press, 1978, 74-100.

able to trivialization as the world became seemingly known and explained on its own terms, while at the same time the scientific informer increasingly ran the risk of becoming the primary, if not the sole, interpretive voice in the world.[4]

This tradition has often left us today with a reactionary heavy-handedness that opts for one informer or the other in our interpretations of the world. From here, the drift into metanarrative configurations becomes a distinct possibility. According to Lyotard, metanarratives fail to deliver a complete and authoritative knowledge of the world and they are hermeneutically and historically deficient as well.[5] Thus, a modernist domination by the one becomes the rule of order that has to face the challenge of being overthrown. However, even when a more open-handed approach is sought, it is not clear how one informer communicates with the other. This dilemma frequently leads to a significant disregard for one of the informers, biblical or scientific, and produces variable degrees of polarization between them.

At this point, we would do well to listen to the salient words of St. Augustine, written long before our knowledge of the world became a potential stumbling block to belief in God, when he said:

> It is not by way of assertion, but by way of inquiry that we have to treat the hidden matters concerning natural things which we know were made by God, the almighty maker. Especially in the books that the authority of God has commended to us, rashness in asserting an uncertain and doubtful opinion scarcely escapes the charge of sacrilege.[6]

---

4 The designation of 'informer' in our hermeneutical strategy carries the connotation that both informers, biblical and scientific, convey 'stories' that the interpreter must contend with. See chapter 1.

5 Lyotard, *The Postmodern Condition: A Report on Knowledge.*

6 St.Augustine on Genesis: *On the Literal interpretation of Genesis: An Unfinished Book,* trans., R. J. Teske, Catholic University Press of America: Wash. D.C., 1991, 45.

Based on this statement, we could conclude that Augustine himself might have concurred with several of the contemporary critiques of metanarrative configurations. Situated at a time when the knowledge of nature was comparatively limited, he already anticipated the need to reign in any exaggerated hermeneutical claims.

The key word in this quote for our study is *inquiry*. Particularly in his work on Genesis, Augustine underscored the importance of taking this inquisitive approach to interpreting Scripture and the natural world. The bishop's poignant words cited above (and in a host of his other writings) encourage interpreters to engage both informers with an open mind.[7] This may partially explain why he made no less than five attempts at interpreting early Genesis without ever coming to conclusions that entirely satisfied him.

One specific issue, among others, that plagued Augustine was whether to interpret the early chapters of Genesis as history, allegory, analogy, or etiology. In attempting to make this determination, he once again relied heavily on his knowledge of the natural world as a valid informer. For Augustine, and by inference for us, remaining open to hermeneutical inquiry was and is a necessary ingredient for avoiding reductionistic tendencies so prevalent in our own day.

We can conclude that in general Augustine's hermeneutical orientation adopted a degree of probing openness between the narrative (biblical) world and the real (natural) world that swerved away from any meta-tight prescriptive formulations of either one.[8] Modifications and re-interpretations of early Genesis were, for Augustine, connected to a network of *refiguring possibilities* that emerged through his ongoing interactions with the stories of the biblical text and his vision of the natural world.

---

7 See chapter 1.

8 See chapter 1 for a fuller discussion of the roles of these informers.

In keeping with this Augustinian tradition, our hermeneutical perspective which we will develop more fully later supports the idea that both the biblical and scientific informers must continuously interact with one another in the unfolding drama of our understanding, explanation, and new understanding of God *and* nature.[9] Since these informers are related, yet distinct, their ongoing dialogue translates into the recognition that an interpretive tension may form between them, just as it did for Augustine. Hence, our knowledge of the world may be different from the Augustinian context, yet our hermeneutical trajectories are similar.

As we approach the creational account in Genesis, we intend to explore three interrelated issues that focus attention on how to better engage with these important chapters. We begin by investigating the peculiar nature of time, which will then prepare us to reflect on narrative and hermeneutics in that order. The application of this three dimensional analysis to the reading of the early Genesis material will allow us to propose a hermeneutical strategy that potentially opens the text up for a more constructive engagement with the world.

Early Visions of Time and a Hermeneutical Arrow

Discussions about the fabric of time and the corresponding temporal aspects of early Genesis and the natural order have a long and interesting history. By turning to look at some of the important earlier visions of time, particularly those of St. Augustine, we intend to gather important insights for our study.

Well before Wordsworth's provocative musings on the enigmatic relationship of concordance, change, and time, Augus-

---

9 See K. J. Vanhoozer, "What is Everyday Theology?" in: *Everyday Theology: How to Read Cultural Texts and Interpret Trends*, Vanhoozer, C. A. Anderson, M. J. Sleasman, eds., Grand Rapids: Baker, 2007, 16, who makes a similar point regarding the engagement with culture.

tine recognized the mysterious nature of time.[10] In a meditation on, 'In the beginning God created the heavens and the earth....' Gen.1:1ff in St. Augustine's *Confessions* Book 11,[11] a fundamental question emerged: 'What, then, is time?'[12] His perplexing response was that he knew well enough, until someone asked him. He longed to understand Genesis and the aporia of time, yet every provisional answer seemed to provoke a new set of questions. To be more explicit, one of his main interests was in the measurement of time. But how can we measure, he asked, that which does not exist.[13] This query indicates that for Augustine the objective nature of time was on shaky ground.

Augustine formed his reply to the questions about time from everyday perceptions: we talk about, calculate, refer to, and are aware of longer and shorter periods of time. Based on these observations he concluded that in both experience and language there is a past, present, and future that correspond to memory, attention, and expectation, respectively. Time, for him, was beginning to be internalized. In Augustine's judgment, the recognition of these temporal/mental associations served as confirmation of the existence or being-ness of time in the face of skepticism's woeful nothing-ness.

In order to formulate this realization, he turned away from any notion of cosmological time and assumed that time was primarily a psychological phenomenon. His configuration of time was built off the idea that there is a threefold present in the soul consisting

---

10 Hawking, *A Brief History*, 8, argues that "the concept of time has no meaning before the beginning of the universe. This was first pointed out by St. Augustine. When asked: What did God do before he created the universe? Augustine didn't reply: He was preparing Hell for people who asked such questions. Instead, he said that time was a property of the universe that God created, and that time did not exist before the beginning of the universe."

11 St. Augstine, *Confessions*, trans., Introduction and Notes, H. Chadwick Oxford: Oxford University Press, 1991, 223. We intend to closely follow Ricoeur's influential work in *Temps et récit I*, Paris: Seuil, 1983, (*Time and Narrative I*).

12 St. Augustine, *Confessions*, Chadwick, 230.

13 Ibid., 231.

of a present past, a present future, and a present present. Hence, for the prolific bishop it is not the creation story in Genesis[14] (although God is understood to be the creator of time), or the movement of heavenly bodies in the theater of the cosmos that allow us to understand and measure time. Rather, the comprehension and experience of time takes place as the mind extracts passive past and future images stored in the soul and converts them into *action-orientated distention possibilities*.[15] This means that temporal distention (distentio) resides in the possibilities associated with the intentional acts of mind: memory, attention, and expectation. To state it more succinctly: mindful intention is deeply anchored in soulful distention. Thus, the present in Augustine's configuration is a psychologically-based present that harbors a cognitively accessible distension to past and future. According to Augustine, not only does this type of distention explain how we measure time, but it also painfully stamps upon us the nature of our being in the world. As he stated the *Confessions* Book 11:

> You are my eternal Father, but I am scattered in times whose order I do not understand. The storms of incoherent events tear to pieces my thoughts, the inmost entrails of my soul, until the day when, purified and molten by the fire of your love, I flow together to merge into you.[16]

Being in the temporal world, says Augustine, is to be disoriented. That is, out of the illusion of the apparent concordance of the *present three-fold present*,[17] there is ultimately and continually a victo-

---

14 The days in Genesis 1, for example, are not particularly important to Augustine. See *Confessions*, 227-228.

15 *Confessions*, 237-240. See also, Ricoeur, *Temps et récit I*, (*Time and Narrative I*, 5-22), who offers pertinent examples and a fuller discussion.

16 *Confessions*, 244.

17 This phraseology captures the Augustinian sense of temporal equilibrium that is achieved between the three elements of temporal experience previously mentioned. Thus, a *'living'* time-oriented present is created that represents *'being'* in the present.

rious discordance. For Augustine, God is eternal and unchanging in contrast to our perplexed and distended temporal existence. Thus, a temporally-driven disjunction exists between us and the Divine, which can be eloquently captured in the terminology of a discordant concordance of time. The final result of this temporal dissimilarity for us is that we are unable to flow into a preferred state of unity with God to whom all is present in the concordance of the same moment.

From this discussion we can appreciate that one of the most remarkable contributions to the aporia of time offered by Augustine was his discovery that its measurement has this discordant – concordant subjective dimension. However, his emphasis on the psychological experience of time polarized the discussion by devaluing the potential role of other complementary perspectives which might deepen our understanding of time's dimensions.

In Augustine's work, both the treatment of time by Genesis and the more objective dimension of time's existence in nature played diminished roles in his understanding. Despite his openness to take each informer into serious consideration, as we highlighted previously, Augustine failed to implement this to a sufficient degree when it came to the problematic of time. His marginalization of Genesis' participation in our comprehension of time and its role in the creation story is particularly striking since time enters the narrative at the very outset of the creation account and continues to run throughout it. John Walton, for example, points out that on day one of the creation week, day (*yom*) is introduced as a period of light and marks the beginning of time.[18] Thus, time is an important first step in the creation of the world, and it sets

---

18 Walton argues that function, not substance was the primary concern of the Hebrews. Accordingly, on Day one of the week of creation (Gen. 1:3-5) "it was not the element of light itself (as physicists would discuss it) that God called *yom*, but the *period* of light" v. 5. By the semantic phenomenon of metonymy, this meaning extends for light ('or) in v. 3 and 4. His conclusion is that God created time on day one. *Ancient Near Eastern Thought and the Old Testament: Introducing the Conceptual World of the Hebrew Bible*, 180.

the stage for a dramatic presentation of the creative unfolding of the rest of the world in time.

When it came to the second perspective, the objective nature of time, Augustine again diminished this side of the temporal equation by giving very little credence to the complex notion of movement and its relationship to time. For many, this was considered a critical aspect of the actual existence of time in the world. To see a greater emphasis on the objective character of time, one need not look any further than Aristotle. He wrestled with the relationship between time and movement as it pertained to the measurement and explanation of time.[19] Aristotle strived to define time from within the cosmological tradition, which stressed that the presence of time shrouds the entire cosmos.[20]

As far as we know today there is no complete explanation of time, but drawing from the resources of both nature and psychology should provide us with a larger tool kit for understanding time. To configure this a bit differently, we might say that natural-cosmological and psychological-lived time, or the objective and subjective nature of time respectively, are related and distinct. That is, while both perspectives need to play a role in synthesizing our understanding of time, there also needs to be resistance toward meta-tendencies that seek to either completely merge or strictly separate their contributions. Consequently, mysteries about time might well persist, but time's peculiar presence will still register through the realities of these mysteries. If this is the case, a relation and distinction configuration does not finally resolve the aporia of time, but it does suggest a way forward; a kind of hermeneutical arrow. To put this in functional terms, both the objective and the subjective elements of time need to act as neces-

---

19 Aristotle, *Physics*, D. Bostock ed., trans., R. Waterfield, New York: Oxford University Press, 2008.

20 Augustine did not entirely deny that movement had some connection to time, yet for all intents and purposes it has little significance for his reflections. See *Confessions*, 237-238.

sary, non-polarizing informers.[21] Hence, thinking about time will always be a complex matter of relation and distinction composed in a dialogical tension that makes every effort to side-step reductionism. [22]

In this section, our objective has not been to resolve the age old problematic of time. Rather, we have simply intended to open up this enigma for further exploration in the context of Augustine's queries. The question at this point in our study is how does time, with its aforementioned complexities, link up with narrative? Later we will connect the discussion of time and narrative into the interpretation of the Genesis creation story.

The Drama of Narrative

Augustine's deliberations over time indicated the importance of this subject to him, though time remained an elusive, if not paradoxical concept in his reflections. Although not entirely mysterious, time's integration into the biblical text, as well as time's relationship to the eternal, proved to defy an unequivocal solution. This lack of resolution may explain why in the end, time was for the most part, absent from his interpretation of these early chapters of Scripture.

Genesis, in Augustine's works, is also referred to as narrative.[23] This awareness however, as was the case for the text's temporal texture, failed to seriously enter into his hermeneutical or exegetical endeavors. In light of the relevant and important focus on the literary dimension of the biblical text today, it would seem appropriate to place a stronger emphasis on the narrative arrangement of early Genesis in order to expand and enhance the hermeneuti-

---

21 See our definition of informer in chapter 1.

22 Hawking, *A Brief History of time*, 145, confirms that attempts to reduce time to a single description are illusory.

23 For example, St. Augustine on Genesis: *On the Literal*, 148-149.

cal inquiry.[24] We contend that a closer inspection of narrative will bring time and narrative in close proximity and that their combined force will help clarify the overall organization and meaning of the creation story.

To begin to get a sense of the dramatic temporal organization of narrative, a detour through the valuable work of Nobel Prize winning author Thomas Mann will prove insightful. In his novel, *The Magic Mountain*, he raises several questions that are relevant to our discussion.[25] Intriguingly, on at least two occasions the author/narrator interrupts the flow of the story to raise queries that echo the struggles of Aristotle, St. Augustine, and Wordsworth concerning time. In Wordsworthian style, Mann, writes: 'What is time? A secret—insubstantial and omnipotent. How does our makeshift assumption of eternity and infinity square with concepts like distance, motion, change, or even the existence of a finite body in space?'[26] Then, later in the story, he poses another challenge, 'Can one narrate time—time as such, in and of itself?'[27]

Mann responds to this query by noting that such an undertaking would have to go something like: time passed, time passed, and time passed. He retorts back that this would be absurd and would clearly fail to resemble narrative. Mann's conclusion is that narrative fills time through action, and that time is the fundamental element in both narration and life. This linkage of narrative with the discussion of the aporia of time raises the perceptive question of whether time and narrative have a deep reciprocal connection to each other.

---

24 H. Blocher, "Biblical Reference and Historical Reference," in: *Scottish Bulletin of Evangelical Theology* 3, (1989), 102-122.

25 T. Mann, *Der Zauberberg. Roman.* Fischer Taschenbuch Verlag: Frankfurt, 1924, *The Magic Mountain*, trans., J. E. Woods, Vintage: New York, 1996.

26 Ibid., 339.

27 Ibid., 531.

At this stage, we refer to Paul Ricoeur who offers a provocative course of action in response to this question in his influential three volume work *Temps et récit* (*Time and Narrative*). In dialogue with the *Confessions* of St. Augustine on time and creatively following Aristotle's *Poetics*, Ricoeur develops the notion that narrative, a creative mimesis (imitation) of action, and the shaping of a plot, which has the capacity to bring together a myriad of moments into a unified and followable story, contributes to enlarging our understanding of time. Narrative, whether fictional or historical, brings about a configuration of time. While fiction is not necessarily concerned with real events in time, in contrast to historiography, both literary modes of story telling fill time.

We do not intend to cover all the details of Ricoeur's thought on this matter, but only to highlight the following general pattern of narrative formation that emerges from his work. According to Ricoeur, the process begins with prefiguration. Prefiguration is rooted in the capacity to identify action and the agent that produces it. At this point, Augustine's notion of distention comes into play and can be grafted onto a phenomenology of action. Ricoeur states:

> What counts here is the way in which everyday praxis orders the present of the future, the present of the past, and the present of the present in terms of one another. For it is this practical articulation that constitutes the most elementary inductor of narrative.[28]

This means that actions in time give rise to and are a conduit for narrative. Thus, prefiguration presupposes a recognition and creative imitation of action and embodies it in terms such as goal or conflict.

Prefiguration is then followed by configuration. Configuration represents a specific literary act of creative mimesis that

---

28 See Ricoeur, *Time and Narrative I*, 60.

generates a story, not a chronology, which consists of a series of actions that are shaped into a dynamic, intelligible, and temporal whole.[29] This unified literary creation expresses a meaningful arrangement, which is formed through the assembly of actions interpreted as significant to the developing story. Ricoeur further argues that the configuring act brings together time and narrative. Configuration, on this account, is thereby able to function as the appropriate vehicle for the reversal of Augustine's discordant concordance depiction of time. In Ricoeur's view, narrative configuration establishes a world of concordant discordance as it draws together a sequence of actions and then shapes them into a temporal unity through the poetic mode of emplotment.[30]

Ricoeur draws the concept of emplotment from Aristotle's *Poetics* and creatively applies it to time and narrative. In typical Ricoeurian fashion, emplotment is the poetic act that mediates through its synergy the concordance and discordance of time. Not only is there a mimetic fusion of actions in narrative (concordance), but there are reversals and surprises that change the course of the story (discordance). This kind of emplotment functions in a poetic mode to construct a narrative time from the energetics of lived and cosmological time. Thus, narrative creates a unique narrative time which is neither a synthesis of lived and cosmological time nor a privileging of one over the other, but rather a negotiation of both time elements in order to function as an imaginary poetic-generating force for the poïesis of a novel and innovative literary configuration.[31]

---

29 Laughery has a fuller discussion in *Living Hermeneutics in Motion: An Analysis and Evaluation of Paul Ricoeur's Contribution to Biblical Hermeneutics.*

30 Ricoeur, *Temps et récit I*, 102. "Bref, la mise en intrigue est l'opération qui tire d'une simple succession une configuration."

31 See chapter 2. Poïesis, we suggested, is the art and action of making saturated phenomena.

To take this narrative configuration a bit further, the dramaturgical Genesis creation story of beginnings recounts in temporal terms a theologically and historically true reality that pertains to its particular subject matter: God and the drama of creation.[32] Time in the early chapters of Genesis has a distinctively theological tone, but this is true only to the extent that lived and cosmological time becomes narrative time in the recounting of the story. Moreover, the biblical author writes from within cosmological and lived time wherein the theological, literary, and historical elements that shape the dramaturgy are preceded by this experience of the world. On the narrative level, therefore, the drama of existential reality is connected to the drama of the manifestation and entry of the revelatory God into time.

In this founding configured narrative, God is depicted as the mighty Creator who takes on the role of the great actor in time and narrative. On this register, the cosmic revelatory drama of God speaking, acting, and proclaiming is to be considered as *sculpting in time*.[33] Understood in these terms, narrative time in Genesis becomes a literary device that negotiates a temporal equilibrium between the eternal and created time with its lived and cosmological features. Accordingly, the narrative is overflowing with action-oriented truth, meaning, and possibilities.

---

32 Following the work of P. Beauchamp in *Création et séparation*, Paris: Desclée, 1969, regarding the structure of the creation narrative, Ricoeur points out: " 'God said,' " "Let there be....," "and there was," "God made," "and God called," "it was the nth day." Note that this chain, running from the stating of an order to the act of execution, is quite comparable to the logic of action of narrative theorists...". See "Sur l'exégèse de Genèse 1:1-2:4," in: *Exégèse et herméneutiqu.* "On the Exegesis of Genesis 1:1-2:4," in: Ricoeur, *Figuring the Sacred: Religion, Narrative, and Imagination*, M. I. Wallace, ed., trans., D. Pellauer, Minneapolis: Fortress, 1995, 136.

33 These picturesque expressions here and in our title are from the magnificent book: A. Tarkovsky, *Sculpting in Time*, trans., K. Hunter-Blair. E. Davis comments that Tarkovsky "thought film's greatest quality as an art form was its ability to capture time and the director's ability to 'sculpt in time." Christianity Today.com, September, 2007.

While there is a revealed dimension of transhistoricity to God's being Creator,[34] God's profound kinship with time, displayed in narrative, life, and the cosmos, provokes a hermeneutical trajectory that subverts any exclusively atemporal or salvific agenda in Genesis.[35] Portrayed as revealing in, through, and beyond time, the Genesis God chisels out the contours of nature and story, and vanquishes all counterfeit claims to creational authority concerning the theodrama of creation.[36]

Returning to Ricoeur's seminal work in *Temps et récit* (*Time and Narrative*) and now going a step further, we arrive at refiguration. When narrative is configured, Ricoeur argues, it becomes a world. This world, among other things, is a world that is offered to be entered, read, and dwelt within, yet this is not to take place without a degree of critical awareness, whereby the reader moves from understanding, through explanation, to new understanding. The act of entering, reading, and dwelling in the configured narrative should be careful to take into consideration the preceding dynamic tasks of prefiguration and configuration, which require that the reader be tuned into the narrative world and not merely his or her own. At this stage, the hermeneutical arc, as Ricoeur

---

34 Interesting parallels between art and narrative: Ricoeur, "Arts, Language and Hermeneutic Aesthetics," An interview by J.-M. Brohm and M. Uhl, September 1996. Our notion of transhistoricity here consists of someone or something that emerges in front of, but also perdures beyond a historical context. For example, think of the biblical text. Like many works of art, it represents, yet escapes being confined to the history of its constitution.

35 Wallace makes the following observations on Ricoeur's chapter, "On the Exegesis of Genesis 1:1-2:4," in: *Figuring the Sacred*, 24-25. Ricoeur's work on Genesis, Wallace states, "isolates the theme of separation as the literary convention that structures the opening creation hymn into a series of dynamic oppositions: order and chaos, night and day, plants and animals," in order to first highlight temporality, the creation itself, and then humanity. This approach stands in contrast to those who underplay time and overplay a salvific centered perspective in the founding Genesis narrative (Augustine, von Rad). From a literary perspective, a Ricoeurian reading, says Wallace, further interprets these early chapters as an "ecological text" where all life forms are ordered into a "cosmic biosphere."

36 Vanhoozer points out, "… we can say that theodramatic understanding calls for a triangulation between words, God's Word, and the world. … The theodrama begins with God bespeaking creation." See "On the Very Idea of a Theological System: An Essay in Triangulating Scripture, Church and World," in: *Always Reforming: Explorations in Systematic Theology*, A.T. B. McGowan, ed., Downers Grove: IVP, 2006, 164-165, also fn. 150. While Vanhoozer's inclusion of the world in this paper is highly encouraging, we are somewhat perplexed about what hermeneutical role it plays in his theological formulations.

refers to it, reaches its full operational potential in moving the reader through time and narrative and in so doing, opening up the possibility of refiguring readerly actions in time.[37]

Reading the early chapters of Genesis as the literary, historical, and poetic theodrama of creation, invites readers to follow the hermeneutical arrow of the story of beginnings towards and through its dynamic re-interpretation. This occurs first of all in the Old Testament itself, and then in the New, and then for the many generations antecedent to ours, and finally to refiguring readers lives today and into the future. This potent theodrama represents a temporally unleashed script that is a legitimate informer about God and nature, which carries the capacity to situate all readers on the stage of the world and to refigure their lives in the name of the Creator.[38]

Neither epic, nor a straight telling of history, the Genesis story of beginnings functions as a founding narrative for the unfolding *drama* of nature and Scripture. Today, the natural world continues to unleash its secrets, discovered through the deliverances of our scientific endeavors; while Scripture continues to create a true world of habitation—a place to dwell, graciously offered through the deliverances of God. Deeply engraved with complexity and mysteriously forged by extravagance, the drama of both narratives presents significant challenges to and for readers, taking us to the limits of imagination.[39]

The Genesis creation drama is therefore transhistorical in that it has the capacity to break out of its immediate cultural context, without denying or effacing it, and to continue to show itself as a story that carries a temporal mark that is fitting for any time. The founding

---

37 Laughery has a fuller discussion in: *Living Hermeneutics*, 131-148.

38 See chapter 2.

39 Vanhoozer, "Pilgrim's Digress: Christian Thinking on and about the Post/Modern Way," in: *Christianity and the Postmodern Turn*, M. B. Penner, ed., Grand Rapids: Brazos, 2005, 71-103, esp. 84. "Stories display the imagination in action, for it is the role of plot (mythos) to unify various persons in a single story with a beginning, middle, and end. The truth of Christianity is not like the universal truths of reason. The cradle of the Christian faith is a story rather than a system."

narrative in Genesis—this story of beginnings, sets out a theological, historical, and literary redescription of the world which stands in stark polemical contrast to other ancient Near Eastern portrayals of creation,[40] as well as to contemporary forms of naturalism.[41]

The Drama of Hermeneutical Re-figurations 'in' Time

What demands further attention, in our view, is the following crucial question: how do the narrative world and the reader's actual/real world address each other? In order to engage this question more fully and before giving our own perspective, we would first like to touch on the recent work of two authors who have been influential in the field of hermeneutics and theology.

Hans Frei's challenging book *The Eclipse of Biblical Narrative*[42] represents an important milestone in biblical hermeneutics. One of his unrelenting points is that Enlightenment thinking established, "a logical distinction and a reflective distance" between the "real historical world" and the "depicted biblical world" (narrative world).[43] This regrettable alienation between the two worlds brought about a reversal of interpretive directions. Frei puts it this way:

> It is no exaggeration to say that all across the theological spectrum the great reversal had taken place; interpretation was a matter of fitting the biblical story into another world with another story rather than incorporating that world into the biblical story.[44]

---

40 Basically, the Genesis account with its strategy to de-deify nature stands alone in its ancient context. See chapter 2.

41 Today, there are a number of voices challenging any credible claims of theism. Authors like Dawkins, *The God Delusion*, Boston: Houghton Mifflin, 2006, and D. Dennett, *Breaking The Spell: Religion as a Natural Phenomenon*, New York: Viking, 2006 are two examples.

42 H. W. Frei, *The Eclipse of Biblical Narrative: A Study in Eighteenth and Nineteenth Century Hermeneutics*, New Haven: Yale University Press, 1974. Also, "The 'Literal Reading' of Biblical Narrative in the Christian Tradition: Does it Stretch or Will it Break?" in: *The Bible and the Narrative Tradition*, F. McConnell, ed., Oxford: Oxford University Press, 1986, 36-77.

43 Frei, *Eclipse*, 5.

44 Ibid., 130.

Thus, the biblical story had been hermeneutically eclipsed and with it, pre-modern literal readings of the Bible began to disappear. As a result of this reversal, the biblical narrative's autonomy and its realistic character were compromised. Frei further notes that:

> In its own right and by itself the biblical story began to fade as the inclusive world whose depiction allowed the reader at the same time to locate himself and his era in the real world rendered by the depiction.[45]

A significant problem that grew out of the Enlightenment environment, as Frei sees it, was that it opened the biblical narrative up to criticism from extra-biblical sources.[46] In his estimation, which to some degree is clearly correct, the effect of this input on the narrative and its reading had a highly corrosive impact.

Take for example the handling of the historical dimension in the biblical material. Frei points out that during the rise of modernism both critics and fundamentalists agreed on the necessity of the referential character of the historical representations in the biblical text. They disagreed, however, on how well the biblical text would hold up to the extra-biblical search light of historical criticism. Critics thought the biblical text would fail to meet the demands of historical veracity behind the text, while the fundamentalists thought otherwise. In Frei's judgment, both camps erred by turning to an extra-biblical source for verification (history), which not only distorted the biblical narrative, but left any realistic (literal, figural) reading of it, in serious jeopardy. What was needed, according to Frei, was a res-

---

45 Ibid., 50.

46 Vanhoozer, *The Drama of Doctrine, A Canonical Linguistic Approach to Christian Theology*, Louisville: Westminster John Knox, 2005, 10. "… Frei demonstrated, perhaps more effectively than anyone else, how biblical critics came to interpret the Bible with frameworks of meaning and criteria of truth that were derived from science, history, and philosophy rather than from Scripture and Christian faith ….. . His own instincts were to let the biblical narrative mean and claim truth on its own terms." Vanhoozer goes on to suggest that Frei never clearly elucidated what "on its own terms" meant.

toration of the biblical narrative to a pristine form that was free from the infiltration of extra-biblical thought and external referential requirements.

His conclusion was that biblical narrative does not refer to actions or events in history, but it refers to itself. What this means is that the biblical narrative is a complete self-contained metanarrative that functions like an autonomous story when it comes to history or any other textual dimension for that matter. Based on this conclusion, the proper hermeneutical action should be one that takes the real world outside the text and draws it into the narrative world inside the text. In other words, the biblical world is *the* inclusive real world.[47] Consequently, a type of *pure narrativism*[48] develops where biblical hermeneutics operates in an extra-biblically free zone, and the biblical narrative appears to be intra-textually static, rather than openly dynamic.

The second author we would like to briefly interact with is John Sailhamer. In his thought provoking *Introduction to Old Testament Theology*,[49] he points out that there are biblical scholars who confuse the real world (events that exist) with the narrative world (a text that reports these events). Failure to recognize this distinction, he argues, plagues biblical hermeneutics. Unlike Frei, Sailhamer is concerned with the historical veracity of the biblical narratives, but he is critical of those who seek to merge the biblical world with the real world of history, archaeology, or perhaps science and philosophy. Such equivalency is problematic for Sailhamer, who states:

---

47 Frei, *Eclipse*, 3.

48 G. L. Comstock, "Truth or Meaning: Ricoeur versus Frei on Biblical Narrative," *JR* 66 (1986), 117-140; "Two Types of Narrative Theology," *JAAR* 55/4 (1987), 687-717.

49 Sailhamer, *An Introduction to Old Testament Theology: A Canonical Approach,* Grand Rapids: Zondervan, 1995. See also, Sailhamer, *The Pentateuch as Narrative* Grand Rapids: Zondervan, 1992.

The narrative world is a fixed reality. It is a function of the narration in the text. The real world is ever-changing and ever-increasing. When one identifies, or equates, the real world and the narrative world as one and the same, the narrative world no longer remains constant. The narrative world changes as we gain more information about the real world. The task of biblical theology is to allow the fixed reality of the narrative world to shape and inform our understanding of the real world, not the other way around.[50]

Thus, Sailhamer has taken the position that the real world and the narrative world are distinct and then sets a hermeneutical arrow in one direction only; that being from the fixed narrative world toward the mutable real world. But can biblical theology ever be informed by the real world, particularly the world that is unleashed by our scientific investigations? Or must Sailhamer's view remain an irreversible hermeneutic trajectory? These queries raise two further questions: 1) what is actually fixed in the narrative world and, 2) is nothing fixed in the real world?

While we applaud the emphasis that both Frei and Sailhamer place on the relevancy of the biblical narrative world, and agree with Sailhamer's point of distinction, we differ with the hermeneutical default mode granted to the narrative world by both authors. As an alternative to these authors' perspectives, our hermeneutical approach calls for a dialogical time-sensitive equilibrium between the real and narrative worlds. Hopefully, the following hermeneutical musings will contribute to the de-eclipsing of biblical narrative.

We intend to briefly examine this kind of interpretive equilibrium between the two worlds in terms of the science and theology debate where the scientific side of the equation functions as a powerful informer about today's real world. It is worth mentioning that prior to the scientific revolution and the consequent

---

50 Sailhamer, *An Introduction to Old Testament Theology*, 36-85, esp. 69-70.

development of our expansive knowledge of the natural world, dialogue between the real and narrative worlds was often viewed as a necessary part of biblical interpretation. Again, Augustine's deliberations about early Genesis, which were cognizant of his knowledge of the natural world, represent a case in point. Therefore, a degree of cooperation between worlds was present in earlier periods of theological development.

Our notion of an interpretive equilibrium is based on several key observations. We begin by acknowledging that the scientific informer has in the past provoked interpretive reconfigurations of the real world that has altered our theological vision (see footnote 4). Likewise on the reverse side of the equation, the biblical narrative world has always presented a disruptive vision of the real world by re-describing it as having meaning and purpose far beyond itself; that is, identified as a creation by a Creative Being. When informed by both worlds, an interpretive balance between the narrative and real world is achieved that leads to novel reconfiguration possibilities. Since the contribution of each informer is contingent on the time, context, and type of question asked, the best configuration in our judgment is a two world dialogue that is comprised of relation and distinction.

That is, to relate the narrative world of early Genesis with the real world may be appropriate in some times and contexts, but call for distinction in others. In our opinion, there is no fixed hermeneutical guarantee that the two worlds will always be related, or that they will always be distinct. This decision can only be made through an ongoing dialogue between the two worlds, which may result in a viable state of tension if and when interpretations collide.[51]

---

51 Hermeneutical hostage taking that automatically favors one world over the other should be critiqued. See P. D. Clayton, *God and Contemporary Science,* Edinburgh: Edinburgh University Press, 1997, 142. While we are sympathetic with Clayton's desire for greater symmetry (and we would add on both sides of the debate), our preference would be for not only more symmetry (relation), but for an important hermeneutical place for dissymmetry (distinction) that will sometimes produce a harmonious result, while at other times it will be left loaded with tension.

Our contention is that the real world should be allowed to shape and inform our understanding, explanation, and new understanding of the narrative world, just as the narrative world does for the real world. Hence, in our hermeneutical configuration, the real world is a necessary and persistent hermeneutical factor that has to be taken into serious consideration when interpreting the narrative world of early Genesis.

If theology is to be biblical, we are hard pressed to see how that is possible without a critical engagement with the real world. Biblical theology, we maintain, is impoverished when it attempts to go it alone or embraces a single arrow trajectory that refuses to acknowledge the real world in time as a valid informer. Thus, practitioners of biblical hermeneutics have to be prepared to deal with changing contexts and real world knowledge that may potentially have an impact on our interpretations of the biblical world.

No better case of this kind of possible hermeneutical reorientation can be found than in the current discussion surrounding human origins. Today, scientific data from anthropology, paleontology, and genetics are coalescing to challenge more traditional interpretations of human origins that are based, for example, on exclusive and literalistic readings of the biblical story of origins.[52] Such readings are frequently characterized by a high degree of hermeneutical closure and produce a corresponding disjunction with the real world as it becomes scientifically known. In contrast, a hermeneutical scenario that favors bidirectional equilibrium and is tuned into the dramatic unfolding of natural knowledge will be open to the real world informer. As a result, some interpretations of the creation account will fall by the wayside simply because

52 For further information about how current knowledge from anthropology and paleontology are impacting theology see Van Huyssteen, *Alone in the World? Human Uniqueness in Science and Theology*, Grand Rapids: Eerdmans, 2006. For further details about how modern genetics is illuminating the picture see for example F. S. Collins, *The Language of God: A Scientist Presents Evidence for Belief*, New York: Free Press, 2006, 133-141.

they have been surpassed, while others will need to be modified, and still others will remain the same.

On the other side of the equation, science needs to move away from its metanarrative tendencies of exclusion in ignoring the biblical world and its creation account of beginnings in Genesis.[53] The scientific informer, as valid to some degree as it may be, has to face the real world and admit its own lack of explanatory power for that which is not less, but far more than empirical data. For example, total comprehension and integration of human uniqueness into our understanding of the world, intuitive and otherwise, and life's fortuitous arrival beg for a wider hermeneutical approach than that offered by atomizing explanations grounded in purely naturalistic perspectives. Openness to the biblical narrative world will go a long ways towards refuting this sort of metanarrative naturalism. When science seeks to go it alone, it not only is unable to justify its own hermeneutical claims to critique-free completeness, but it misses the opportune target of a wider equilibrium in reality itself by limiting the direction of the hermeneutical arrow.

Conclusion

In thinking about the inexhaustible resources that time and change present to our imagination, we are drawn back to our poetic starting point. Wordsworth's poem attempted to grasp the ungraspable. The elusive nature of time and its relationship to change was recognized well before Wordsworth by notable figures like Augustine. Even though Augustine realized the importance

---

53 Vanhoozer in *Everyday Theology*, 38, is rightly concerned to preserve meaning over against a reductionist ("nothing but") sociobiological constructivism, and to argue for a necessary distinction between the biblical world and the real world informers. While we concur with the general tenor of Vanhoozer's critique of reductionism and his emphasis on the *more than this*, it will at times, do us well to remember the possibility of affirming the *not less than this* when it is truly testified to in the real world.

of this discussion, he failed to identify the full potential that the Genesis narrative might hold for illuminating our understanding of time. We argued, following the thought of Ricoeur, that narrative time in early Genesis broadens our perspectives and deepens our perceptions of time, God, and nature as it mediates between lived and cosmological time. Furthermore, we put forward the notion that in its role as a founding narrative, early Genesis functions as a reflective backdrop that opens up our hermeneutical horizon to the possibilities of an unfolding theological, historical, and literary re-description of the world. By framing the discussion in this way, our re-descriptions are sensitive to our changing knowledge about the world. This led us to the conclusion that, in contrast to Frei and Sailhamer, there is a hermeneutical necessity that requires the narrative-time world and the real-time world to interact as legitimate informers. Thus, in the final analysis these informers have the potential to shape each other, which reinforces the dynamic, changing nature of the dialogue between science and theology.

As readers of the Genesis creation story today we must realize that we are foreigners to the text and its ancient Near Eastern context, yet we are not excluded from engaging with its God, time, narration, and drama in a refractive spherical pattern. Refigured lives in time then become a real possibility for those readers who are grafted into the revelatory story of God's sculpting in time, both through creation and the ever-present redemptive outpouring of love in Christ, which graciously offers a place and a role on the stage of the cosmic drama still in progress. This poetic and theologically-loaded biblical world drama not only includes a narrative concordance that supersedes discordance with respect to time or changing portraits of the real world, but it also proclaims that life triumphs over death and will continue to do so throughout God's ongoing story.

EXPLORING THE POSSIBLE WORLD OF GENESIS 2-3

WITH PAUL RICOEUR

We shall not cease from exploration
And the end of our exploring
Will be to arrive where we started
And know the place for the first time

These salient words from TS Eliot in the Four Quartets set the tone for this chapter. Poets, like Eliot, have ways with words that configure worlds and how we view them. Thus, they are creators of powerful images of innovation and impertinence, which careen off the walls of time and sweep over the landscape of life, calling us to re-envision where we started. Engaging in the intricate and inquisitive art of exploration is a perpetual challenge, which comes to an end with a new perception of the beginning.

The work of Paul Ricoeur has received wide acclaim for its thought-provoking contribution to a diverse set of topics, including contemporary hermeneutics, philosophy, and theology. Undeniably, landmark publications like *Time and Narrative* and *The Symbolism of Evil*, as well as many others, have strongly impacted a number of disciplines within the academic community. When one considers his extensive list of publications, as well as the integrative complexity of his thoughts, it seems likely that Ricoeur's ideas could play a more significant role in a variety of discussions today. Not only did his exploration of the critical relationships of time, narrative, and history, enable us to better appreciate what constitutes the biblical story, but his developments in hermeneutics has the capacity to blaze a path forward whenever interpretations within and between disciplines collide and conflict.

One of the most significant debates in today's marketplace of ideas is taking place between science and theology: stories of beginnings. Notably, data streaming in from various academic disciplines, ranging from genomics to the neurosciences, is painting a powerful naturalistic and evolutionary portrait of human origins. While the discussion of human evolution is not new, the information supporting it has strengthened considerably and serves to quicken our awareness of the theological implications of accommodating this perspective.[1] Consequently, the interpretation of many crucial biblical passages is undergoing reassessment. In particular, as the realization of humanity's evolutionary past solidifies, it casts an increasingly long shadow on the interpretation of Genesis 2-3. The basic hermeneutical question for this text becomes: how might it be configured today so that it remains a viable informer about God, humanity, and the world? The threat of conflict between science and Scripture at this point is high and has the potential to spill over and challenge a broad spectrum of

---

1   J. F. Haught, *Making Sense of Evolution: Darwin, God, and the Drama of Life*, Louisville: John Knox Press, 2010, xv, draws attention to the theological fallout of evolutionary science when he states that "Although many Christians still try to escape or ignore Darwin's message, his revolutionary and ragged vision of life will eventually have to be taken into account in any realistic theological understanding of God, the natural world, life, human identity, morality, sin, death, redemption, and the meaning of our lives."

theological thinking. Where does this leave us as interpreters of the world and the text?

In general, the potential for conflict raises the perennial question of how much our knowledge of the world should influence biblical interpretation. It is a reminder that general hermeneutical strategies need to be in place before approaching more specific questions. Our previous chapters made the point that in order to attain optimal understanding an interpretive equilibrium had to be reached between informers, notably the biblical and scientific ones.[2] This means that as our interpretive gaze shifts from one informer to the other, the complementary actions of challenge and critique will take center stage. While initially destabilizing, these actions can serve as keys for unlocking new possibilities for viewing the past, present, and future. As a result, prior interpretations may fade into obsolescence, as one's increasing knowledge of the world unfolds. In the final analysis then, the question for Genesis 2-3 becomes: is there a hermeneutical strategy for this text that allows it to accommodate a global evolutionary perspective with its changing portraits of human nature?

In an attempt to be open to both the scientific and biblical worlds and in order to come to a better, albeit negotiated understanding of Genesis 2-3, we will explore the work of Paul Ricoeur.[3] Inasmuch as his influence has only touched the margins of the science and theology discussion, there is room for a constructive development of his thought in this type of discourse. Thus, the study is organized around four Ricoeurian themes: 1) the nature of symbol and myth, 2) hermeneutics, 3) the dynamic relationship between time, narrative and history, and 4) the separation motif.

---

2   See Chapters 1-3.

3   For theologically oriented works by Ricoeur consult, *History and Truth*, Bloomington: Northwestern University Press, 1955; *Essays on Biblical Interpretation*, Minneapolis: Fortress, 1980; *Figuring the Sacred*, Minneapolis: Fortress, 1995; Ricoeur and A. LaCocque, *Thinking Biblically*, Chicago: University of Chicago Press, 1998. See also, Laughery, *Living Hermeneutics in Motion: An Analysis and Evaluation of Paul Ricoeur's Contribution to Biblical Hermeneutics*.

Symbol and Myth: The Architecture of Explorative Thought

One of the most impressive features of human thought is the ability to create and configure symbols in an effort to express meaning. Early in his career, Ricoeur took note of this phenomenon with the publication of *The Symbolism of Evil*.[4] In this book, he explored the meaning of archaic symbols, principally those he found in Genesis 2-3. It was at this point in his work that a number of ideas were beginning to coalesce; ideas that would ultimately affect his view of the symbolic. In particular, he realized that phenomenology (the study of describing conscious experience) could not operate without hermeneutics.[5] This meant that it was impossible to have direct access to the ontology of understanding finite being. According to Ricoeur, this could only be approached indirectly by first traversing the symbols expressed, notably in texts, through the fields of language, semantics, linguistics, and reflective thought.

By making this long detour, he was able to expound an epistemology of interpretation, built on the ontology of understanding, but going beyond it and this led to the idea that hermeneutics should be grafted onto phenomenology.[6] In other words, symbols and text interpretation play a primordial role in understanding and depicting experience.[7] This alternative route effectively expanded and radically impacted the Ricoeurian notion of human existence. Consequently, he now saw symbols, especially those embedded in the biblical text, as able to reveal *God and being in the world* in *polyphonic ways*. Ricoeur further emphasized that

---

4 Ricoeur, *The Symbolism of Evil*.

5 Since the hermeneutic problem; the exegesis and understanding of a text precedes phenomenology, Ricoeur argues it cannot be set aside or ignored. See *The Conflict of Interpretations, Essays in Hermeneutics*, D. Ihde ed., Evanston: Northwestern University Press, 1974, 3-26.

6 Ibid. 3-26.

7 Ibid. Ricoeur is concerned to make room for language, method, and epistemology when it comes to understanding text, self, and world.

there was a fundamental linkage between language and symbols, which led him to propose the following series of connections: being human is connected to language, which is connected to reflection, which is connected to interpretation. Out of this intellectual brew was born the infamous maxim: 'the symbol gives rise to thought'. For Ricoeur, the text became the primary site where symbol, thought, and interpretation merged. This train of thought strongly reinforced the premise that the nature of *being* in the world *is* hermeneutical; i.e., interpretation *is* ontological and epistemological. From this point on, his massive body of work unfolded in a hermeneutically sensitive manner.

Based on the previous discussion, one can understand why Ricoeur would assume a posture in *The Symbolism of Evil* that there is no direct or immediate access to evil.[8] Therefore, any accounting of evil can only be obtained through the interpretation of signs, symbols, and myths. Naturally, this thesis drove him to look more closely at the Genesis 2-3 narrative. However, before beginning to address this passage, one can ask the general question: how does the symbol lead to the deciphering and decoding of something like evil? According to Ricoeur, it does so through the hermeneutic endeavor of understanding the symbol as a mediating expression between experience and reflection, which for evil is rooted in the language of defilement, sin, and guilt.[9] From this perspective, the symbolic can be seen as that which evokes imaginative thought and carries meaning that reaches beyond one's total comprehension. In a sense, the symbol transcends what can be known. As Ricoeur states:

---

8 "First of all, my investigation into the *Symbolism of Evil*, which followed upon *The Voluntary and the Involuntary* and *Fallible Man*, carried me to the heart of the hermeneutical tradition. For in the case of evil there is no direct concept but, to begin with, symbols, narratives, myths, instead." See Ricoeur, "My Relation to the History of Philosophy," *The Iliff Review* 35 (1978), 9.

9 Ricoeur refers to this as a phenomenology of confession; the confession of evil in man. See *The Symbolism of Evil*, 4-5.

I readily grant today that the interpretation of symbols is not the whole of hermeneutics, but I continue to hold that it is the condensation point and, if I may say so, the place of the greatest density, because it is in the symbol that language is revealed in its strongest force and with its greatest fullness. It says something independent of me, and it says more than I can understand. The symbol is surely the privileged place of the experience of the surplus of meaning.[10]

As an *augmentation* of reality, symbols carry the potential to expand the interpretative space and give rise to an outpouring of meaning. As a result, symbols form the means to encode and promote explorative thought and thereby, open up a realm of creative possibilities for reflection.

It is important to note that when Ricoeur talks about a 'surplus of meaning,' he does not mean a 'whatever meaning suits the interpreter meaning.' Rather, he is saying that even though symbols have extensive meaning, they still operate within a given domain. Without these constraints, the symbol would be incomprehensible. What this means practically is that the interpretation and understanding of symbols revolves around their connections to realities in the living world. However, this measure of hermeneutical realism does not limit the reflective potency of the symbolic.[11]

These ideas lead to one of the major questions of this paper: how do symbols, particularly sacred ones, go about interacting with human thought? According to Ricoeur, the symbolic sphere functions in a theoretical space composed of cosmic, psychic, and poetic dimensions.[12] The pattern of symbolic formulation begins with a first order reading of the sacred onto the world that is then spoken into symbol, thereby empowering it to refer to the mani-

---

10 Ihde, *Hermeneutic Phenomenology*, Evanston: Northwestern University Press, 1971, xvi-xvii. See Ricoeur, Foreword.

11 D. R. Stiver, *Theology After Ricoeur: New Directions in Hermeneutical Theology*, Louisville: Westminster John Knox, 2001, 94-97.

12 Ricoeur, *The Symbolism of Evil*, 10.

festations of the sacred that started the cycle in the first place. This circular movement is often attached to conspicuous elements in the natural world, like the sun, moon, and sky, to form the most basic cosmic symbols. These cosmic symbols often became expressed in ancient myths and rituals. Therefore, these sanctified cosmic realities function as *meaning manifestors* for language that signifies a variety of expressions ranging from the identity of the divine to wonder, fear, and order. The other two dimensions run alongside the cosmic one. The psychic dimension recognizes that cosmic elements emit reflections that enter one's thoughts through dreams and internal self understanding, and the poetic dimension recognizes that various cosmic resonances eventually translate into the language of theology and being. This operational bandwidth of the symbolic provides the inertia for aligning humanity's being with the sacred.

To turn the discussion toward the topic of myth,[13] one can ask the question: what connection exists between myth and symbol? Ricoeur starts by noting that the revealing power of symbols forms the primary matter for myth. What he means by this is that the creation of myth emerges out of symbol interpretation. In Ricoeur's thinking, when interpreted symbols develop into mythical narra-

---

[13] We are aware that the notion of myth is complex, and are attuned to the problem of a polyphony of meanings. See G. B. Caird, *The Language and Imagery of the Bible*, Philadelphia: Westminster, 1980, 219-242, who delightfully refers to myth as an "exceedingly slippery term." He also argues that, "myths are stories about the past which embody and express a people's traditional culture." Vanhoozer, *Remythologizing Theology: Divine Action, Passion, and Authorship*, Cambridge: Cambridge University Press, 2010, 3-5, offers a brief, but pertinent discussion of myth, "the term oscillates uneasily between 'foolish delusion' and 'vehicle of higher truth'." He goes on to point out: "Myths are 'sacred stories' or 'stories of the gods' that characteristically take place in sacred space-time (i.e. apart from the reality of ordinary history) and typically involve superhuman speech and acts. Myths may have an explanatory function (as a stand-in for science), an illustrative function (as a stand-in for philosophy), or a communal function (as a foundation narrative that shapes a group's identity)." Concerning the language of myth in biblical literature, N. T. Wright, *The New Testament and the People of God*, London: SPCK, 1992, 424-427, states: "However foreign to post-Enlightenment thought it may be to see meaning within history, such language grows out of Israel's basic monotheistic and covenantal theology." It is important to underscore that for Ricoeur myth is "not a false explanation by means of image and fable, but a traditional narration which relates to events that happened at the beginning of time .... ." and then applies to today. Myth, therefore does not, according to Ricoeur, aim to *explain* per se, but it sets out to offer an *exploratory* significance and a contribution to understanding. See *The Symbolism of Evil*, 5.

tives, they have the capacity to point us down a path of discovery and revelation concerning the relationship of humanity with the sacred.[14] Myth is thought to carry a fuller meaning than 'history', because myth is not constrained by a precise data-like presentation of what happened, where it happened, and when it happened. Since this is the case, narrated myth's poetic sphere with its more expansive space and time elements will not mirror the external world.[15] Narrated myth, therefore, frees up the discourse from limiting exactitude, whether geographical, historical, or otherwise, and spurs on our imaginative efforts.[16] The world of myth, then, can reach well beyond mundane constraints to establish foundations for being and meaning. Consequently, mythic configurations open up the hermeneutical horizon so that meaningful contacts with hard to grasp realities, like the beginning of time, are engendered. As an aside, these Ricoeurian ideas point to the fact that relying solely on critical historical methods for unpacking a text with mythic-like resonances will fall woefully short of the mark.[17]

At this point, two observations can be made that will resonate in the discussion as it moves forward. First, myth-like constructions consist of a network of interpreted symbols. This means that

---

14 Ricoeur, *The Symbolism of Evil*, 5.

15 While there are different perspectives of the notion of poetic, Ricoeur puts it this way: "Par poétique, j'entends quelque chose de plus riche que simplement la poésie rythmée ou rimée, une certaine création de sens, mobilisant des formes du discours, des jeux de langage autres que la description factuelle et aboutissant à des compositions, des configurations en forme d'œuvres identifiables en termes de catégories littéraires distinctes et plus ou moins stables." "Herméneutique: Les finalités de l'exégèse biblique," in: *La bible en philosophie*, Paris: Cerf, 1993, 27-51. By poetic, I mean something richer than simply rhythmic or rhyming poetry - a certain creation of meaning, that mobilizes forms of discourse, language games other than factual description and that culminates in compositions, configurations in the form of identifiable works in terms of distinct literary categories that are more or less stable. (GJL's translation).

16 Some argue that myth and story can be bearers of a truth and reality, which are tethered to, but go far beyond our everyday empirical observations. Creating literary worlds is apt to be a valuable enterprise for telling it like it really is. J. R. R. Tolkien, "On Fairy Stories," in: *The Tolkien Reader*, New York: Ballantine, 1966, 33-99 and C. S. Lewis, "On Stories," in: *Of This and Other Worlds*, Walter Hooper, ed., London: Collins, 1982, 25-45 and "Myth Became Fact," in: *God in the Dock*, W. Hooper, ed., Grand Rapids: Eerdmans, 1990, 63-67.

17 Ricoeur, *The Symbolism of Evil*, 18. For a range of perspectives on myth and the Hebrew Bible, see *Myth, Ritual, and Kingship*, S. H. Hooke ed., Oxford: Clarendon, 1958, and *Philosophy, Religious Studies, and Myth*, R. A. Segal ed., New York: Garland, 1996.

myth can give rise to an orchestrated cluster of thoughts about God and the world. Thus, this type of construction can function well in an exploratory mode, making it aptly suited for probing the mysteries of the deep past. To take this a bit further, it could be said that interpreted symbols provide the architectural support and integral hardware for narrating a possible picture of the beginning of time. Second, myth is a configuration that originates from lived experience, and though it should not be construed as 'history' as described above, it nonetheless has valid meaning and a bearing on history.[18] Hence, myth can resemble traditional narration in some respects, as it presents a story of beginnings that is tuned into the cultural climate of its time. If the Genesis 2-3 narrative has mythic-like dimensions, or at least is heavily dominated by mythical features, it should exhibit a high degree of correspondence with these observations.[19]

In coming to a decision of what description best fits Genesis 2-3, Ricoeur examined four categories of myth regarding the origin and end of evil. First, beginning with the most ancient, there is the drama of creation found in Sumerian—Akkadian texts. In these texts, battles with primeval chaos dominate, and evil is a constant presence to be overcome. Second, there are tragedies. Notably, Greek myths often present humans and gods in opposition, whereby the theme of a "blinded" humanity faces the pending doom of the capricious gods and their potentially evil intents. The third category is that of the exiled soul with its division of humanity into body and soul where the body, viewed as evil, needs to be overcome to re-join a divine soul. Lastly, there is an eschatological or anthropological category. This, for Ricoeur, is where Genesis 2-3 fits in best. Whereas the first three categories present a picture

---

18 See chapter 2.

19 Primeval stories may have been thought to have happened, but in a different although somewhat recognizable world, compared to the reader's own. See T. Stordalen, *Echoes of Eden: Genesis 2-3 and the Symbolism of the Eden Garden in Biblical Hebrew Literature*, Leuven: Peeters, 2000, esp. 66.

of evil as belonging in the world from the very outset, the biblical account is different. It presents, according to Ricoeur, a radical separation between the origin of good and the origin of evil. That is, primeval creation began as something fundamentally good and only secondarily became tarnished through the malice lurking in the form of a talking serpent and the subsequent response of the human pair. Evil, therefore, is given a temporal beginning that becomes part of the unfolding drama of human history.

What then can be made of this opening volley with Paul Ricoeur? First, it is safe to say that the Genesis 2-3 narrative is teeming with vibrant symbolism. Powerful imagery like the Divine act of sculpting man from the ground, a talking serpent, and magical trees dominate the architecture of the story. Attempting to put this forward as actual occurrences in the past will strongly clash with evolutionary history and our scientific understanding of the natural world. While not always wanting scientific ideas to dictate the terms of the discussion, they nonetheless are a significant informer that can contribute to our understanding and provide critical insights into the nature of this biblical narrative. For example, the curse that doomed serpents to a lifetime of crawling on the ground strongly conflicts with science. Scientific studies have dated fossil remains of these crawling reptiles as far back as 100 million years ago or more.[20]

What does this incongruity mean? First, it highlights the notion that the ancient Hebrews had very limited access to the deep past; second, it emphasizes that Genesis 2-3 is a highly symbolic narrative. To expand the second point further, symbols like clever serpents, an extravagant garden, and plants of life have significant parallels with other ancient Near Eastern stories. In addition, there is solid biblical scholarship showing that sanctuary symbol-

---

20 N. Vidal, J. Rage, A. Couloux, and S. B. Hedges, 'Snakes (Serpentes),' in: *The Timetree of Life*, S. B Hedges and S. Kumar, eds., Oxford: Oxford University Press, 2009, 390-397.

ism is woven into the fabric of the narrative.[21] These contextual observations reinforce the conclusion that Genesis 2-3 is a powerful symbolic narrative. To classify it as a chronicle-like description of literal events would neuter its thought-provoking force and move it out of alignment with its context.

Further reflection about the connection between symbols and text brings us to another conclusion. It has already been pointed out that symbols could provide the support structure from which to launch a thoughtful exploration into relatively unknown territory, like the beginning of time. In other words, it opens up possibilities for engagement with a hard to grasp past. Might this be the case for the Genesis 2-3 narrative? This is an important question that will remain in the forefront as the study progresses. But for now, one other suggestion can be offered that could signal the merit of this approach to the text. Many readers assume that the biblical author had fairly complete resolution on theological matters and possessed significant knowledge about precisely what happened in the distant past. However, this is probably not the case. For example, when it comes to evil, the biblical author—like many of us—very likely did not know how to resolve the conflict between the presence of evil in the world and God's reign over it. In early Genesis, God is portrayed as having ultimate authority over the world, yet evil lurks in the background. Notice that this dilemma begins to present itself with the arrival of a wily serpent that is already equipped with the intent and skill to counter the

---

21 For valuable insights on this symbolic landscape see, Wenham, "Sanctuary Symbolism in the Garden of Eden Story," in: *I Studied Inscriptions from Before the Flood: Ancient Near Eastern, Literary, and Linguistic Approaches to Genesis 1-11*, 399-404. G. K. Beale, *The Temple and the Church's Mission: A Biblical Theology of the Dwelling Place of God*, Downers Grove: IVP, 2004, and "Eden, the Temple, and the Church's Mission in New Creation," *Evangelical Theological Society* 48/1 (2005), 5-31. J. Morrow, "Creation as Temple-Building and Work as Liturgy in Genesis 1-3," *Journal of the Orthodox Center for the Advancement of Biblical Studies* (2009), 1-13. Wenham, Beale, and Morrow contend that there are numerous features of temple/sanctuary imagery found in Gen. 2-3. They argue that these reflect the symbolization of the Garden of Eden as a cosmic temple – the archetypal sanctuary, wherein God was present. Beale's further suggestion (66-80) that Eden was "the first temple, upon which all of Israel's temples were based" seems, in our view, to get the trajectory the wrong way around. That is, temple/sanctuary imagery in this narrative is more likely to flow back into the story, rather than out from it.

Creator (Gen. 3:1). This description may reflect the irreconcilable mystery of the existence of evil and Divine authority. On the one hand, God's authority is expressed by creating the serpent crafty and readied for its dirty work; while on the other hand, His intolerance of evil is expressed with the subsequent condemnation of the serpent's inevitable actions. Neither resolves the conundrum, but merely expresses it. Does this puzzling picture indicate anything about the nature of the story? It does fit with an interpretation of Genesis 2-3 that recognizes the exploratory nature of the text. This might explain, for example, why nothing in the story is overtly called evil. Perhaps, the narrative is more about *who* is in the beginning and less about the origin of evil.

In concluding this section, one final comment needs to be made about Ricoeur's classification scheme. As pointed out earlier, he leans strongly in the direction of an ontological – anthropological interpretation of Genesis 2-3. While this makes sense to a degree, it may be too reductionistic. For example, there are significant theological concerns arising from life in the ancient Hebrew world that appear to be driving the itinerary of the narrative. This primeval account is clearly connected to the unfolding history of Israel despite any challenge to the literal veracity of the story. Upon further consideration, it seems likely that the text does not fit comfortably into any one of the four Ricoeurian categories.

The question remains: is Genesis 2-3 myth? For now, the answer is yes and no. What might be said at this point is that the narrative mimic's myth in many ways, but it is not a carbon copy. After all, the main character is Yahweh who the Israelites knew was active in their corporate life and being the one and only God, must have been active at the beginning of time. Hence, the theological and historical realities of ancient Hebrew life were bound to become reflected in the text. Naturally, the ancient Hebrews would have viewed their story of creation quite differently from the surrounding culture's myths of creation. No doubt, the biblical account of beginnings formed a strong and *measured* contrast with the other stories of beginnings, rendering them counterfeit. Based on these kinds of differences, it seems safe to question whether or not Genesis 2-3 fits cleanly into the myth category, regardless of similarities.

Hermeneutics: The Artistry of Weaving Thoughts

Several introductory claims about the nature of hermeneutics need to be made at the outset. First, the general action of interpreting anything is part and parcel of what it means to be a human being encountering and coming to know the world. Second, the interpretive act is a hard wired neural function that enables the quest for optimal understanding. Third, this quest can be viewed as a circuitous passage that takes one through different kinds of worlds: spiritual, natural, contextual, textual, and otherwise. Fourth, along the journey, thoughts of various types—including discordant ones—are garnered and woven together into a reflective concordant whole. It might be said this way: our overall picture of the world condenses out of the mist of a life being experienced. Hence, the base-line level of being in the world must incorporate this hermeneutical dimension. Fifth, once the significance of this dimension is acknowledged, it leads to the conclusion that value free, unbiased assessments of any kind of data are impossible. This makes presuppositions, context, and unique historical circumstances significant factors that must weigh heavily on any interpretation.

It is imperative to state that this five-point description of hermeneutical actions should apply with equal force to the biblical writer of Genesis 2-3. In other words, the biblical author was first and foremost an interpreter himself who sought to grasp the significance of God's interactions with the ancient Hebrew people, the world, and humanity in general. Most significantly then, the biblical writer lived and wrote within the confines of a contextually situated *hermeneutical web of life*, which would have shaped the kinds of connections he made with the cosmos and its Divine architect, the living God of Israel.[22]

Hermeneutics was central to the thinking of Paul Ricoeur. He was one of the most influential voices in the twentieth century on the topic as he promoted the significance of both general and more selective (regional) hermeneutical strategies. In an academic environment where general hermeneutics was becoming the dominant philosophical theory of understanding, he set out to re-establish that language and, therefore, texts are fundamental features of the hermeneutical task.[23] This theoretical move re-routed hermeneutics so that it could link into epistemology. By coupling interpretation to knowledge, he developed an *epistemology of interpretation* that was couched in a way of being.[24] Thus, the rigor and practice of epistemology cannot be ignored or blended into ontology as knowledge is always in dialogue with being through the dynamics of language and the interpretation of texts.[25]

As a result, the text for Ricoeur was put into interpretive motion as part of what he called the hermeneutical arc of understanding and explanation. In this arc, the primary focus of hermeneutics became the discernment of the 'matter' of the text. From here, the text with its interpretive portfolio entered into a hermeneutical space of wide reflective dialogue. It is in this space that Ricoeur saw that the text can modify one's overall understanding of the world. Thus, in our view, texts harbor the ability to move us

---

22 Smith, *The Fall of Interpretation: Philosophical Foundations for a Creational Hermeneutic.*

23 While biblical interpretation seems to initially function in the regional sphere, Ricoeur points out that, "Theological hermeneutics presents features that are so original that the relation is gradually inverted, and theological hermeneutics finally subordinates philosophical hermeneutics to itself as its own organon." See "Philosophical and Biblical Hermeneutics," in: *From Text to Action, Essays in Hermeneutics II*, 89-101, especially 90.

24 Ricoeur, "The Task of Hermeneutics," in: *From Text to Action*, 53-74.

25 Ibid., Especially 69. Interacting principally with Heidegger's philosophy, especially in *Being and Time*, Ricoeur argues, "Now a philosophy that breaks dialogue with the sciences is no longer addressed to anything but itself." Properly epistemological questions in Heidegger's work, according to Ricoeur, are problematically left aside.

from understanding to new understanding through what is said in discourse fixed by writing. While we applaud the emphasis Ricoeur places on the text as a hermeneutical factor, it needs to be pointed out that discerning the matter of the text cannot be done in isolation. Interpretation of the text operates within the wider sphere of the knowledge and understanding of the world and thereby, is affected by such knowledge and understanding.[26] From an epistemological point of view, there is a hermeneutical circle that can shift, but not be broken.

What led Ricoeur to many of his insights was the recognition that hermeneutics could not be solely concerned with the interpretation of symbols. He broadened his understanding of hermeneutics with the examination of metaphor (*The Rule of Metaphor*), narrative (*Time and Narrative*), and the Bible (*Essays in Biblical Interpretation*).[27] One of the most remarkable features of metaphor and narrative underscored in these studies is what he referred to as a *semantic impertinence.* That is, the sentence (metaphor) or story (narrative) is filled with tension on the literal level, which demands that the reader go further to connect with a surplus of meaning already operative in symbols.[28]

The metaphorical extravagance of the Genesis 2-3 narrative makes it a prime candidate to fit into this configuration at several levels. Take, for example, the talking snake; the hermeneutical serpent of chapter 3 who reinterprets the Divine directive.[29] Everyone knows from experience that snakes are incapable of speech or

---

26 Laughery, *Living Hermeneutics*, 131-148.

27 "What is essential in the case of narrative discourse is the emphasis on the founding event or events as the imprint, mark, or trace of God's act. God's mark is in history before being in speech." Ricoeur, "Towards a Hermeneutic of the Idea of Revelation," *Essays on Biblical Interpretation*, 73-118. Also, Laughery, *Living Hermeneutics*, 105-128.

28 Ricoeur, *Interpretation Theory: Discourse and the Surplus of Meaning*, Fort Worth: Texas Christian University Press, 1976, 50-55, where he points out that a Wordsworth poem about a sunrise "signifies more than a meteorological phenomenon."

29 Beauchamp, "Le serpente herméneute," in: *L'Un et L'Autre Testament, vol. 2*, Paris: Seuil, 1990, 137-158. See also, M. Emmrich, "The Temptation Narrative of Genesis 3 :1-6 : A Prélude to the Pentateuch and the History of Israel," *Evangelical Quarterly* 73 1 (2001), 3-20.

any thoughts related to speech, so injecting this element into the narrative shocks the reader's sensibilities and drives our hermeneutical networks to question and look for more. In other words, two quite different worlds confront each other—a natural world with crawling, reflexive reptiles and an exotic world with thinking, speaking serpentine beings. The discordance clearly elevates the level of interpretive tension and raises a host of questions. For instance, how can these two worlds possibly interact and jointly influence our interpretation of the actual world? Furthermore, how does this metaphorical extravagance affect the interpretation of Genesis 2-3?

Continuing with Ricoeur, he further elaborated the hermeneutical role of metaphors and narratives by describing them as *semantic innovations* that have the potential to offer a *re-description of reality*.[30] Clearly, Genesis 2-3 is a dramatic re-visioning of reality with its theo-poetic[31] depiction of the world that is related to, yet distinct from our experience and knowledge of the natural world.[32] This radical re-description represents an interpretation of reality where metaphorical innovation, thought-provoking tension, and reflection rule. This re-visioning does not consist of a mere recitation of natural phenomena for the sake of empirical accuracy. As a theo-poetic re-description, which in many ways is out of sync with our knowledge of the natural world, it does not necessarily stand in opposition to a scientific vision of it. Rather,

---

30 Ricoeur, *Interpretation Theory*, 66-68. Also, *Time and Narrative, I*, Chicago: University of Chicago Press, 1984, 81. R. P. Scharlemann, "The Textuality of Texts," in: *Meaning in Texts and Actions: Questioning Paul Ricoeur*, D. E. Klemm and W. Schweiker, eds., Charlottesville: University Press of Virginia, 1993, 13-25.

31 This (original?) metaphor attempts to underscore that Gen. 2-3 is a theological poetic text, not merely a poetic one, which is in keeping with chapters 1-3. See also, Laughery, *Living Hermeneutics*, 46-56, who argues that Ricoeur takes a similar position.

32 C. G. Bartholomew and R. P. O'Dowd, *Old Testament Wisdom Literature: A Theological Introduction*, Downers Grove: IVP, 2011, 68-72, insist that metaphors, stories, and poems are essential elements for connecting – bridging the gap between, "…. God's power and goodness and the strangeness of everyday life." Wisdom, being deeply rooted in creation, invites us to see the world anew and calls for the recovery of biblical literature, more precisely its poetry, to open our horizons in surpassing the fixed, calculated, and quantified.

being unbounded, it can function symbiotically with an empirically-based understanding and open up the hermeneutical horizon to creative possibilities.

Based on the hermeneutically-oriented work of Paul Ricoeur, it is clear that the reader of the biblical text must be wary of overly simplistic approaches to the interpretation of Genesis 2-3. But it is important to add that the same holds true for the scientific side. The scientific enterprise creates its own world with its own empirically-based narratives of the natural world that are not free from similar hermeneutical considerations. When the scientific world simply dismisses Genesis 2-3 as an empirically defective account, it fails to grasp the integrative hermeneutical significance of a jarring theo-poetic re-description of reality.[33] If it was never intended to have empirical veracity and air-tight correspondence with the natural world, for example, it cannot be judged on those grounds. Ricoeur has alerted us to the hermeneutical reality that texts, including biblical texts like Genesis 2-3, are a hermeneutical force.

Time, Narrative, and History: Putting Thoughts into *World* Patterns

To begin this section, it is intriguing to note what the neurosciences are revealing about how the human brain works. It is increasingly clear that one of the things at the core of brain function is the ability to form and create narratives.[34] Our brains automatically build and fill in stories to infuse our lives with meaning, purpose, and direction, rendering narrative an effective vehicle for constructive thought and communication. One effect of this narrative impulse is that our minds build *cognitive worlds* that can be thoughtfully entered, reflected on, and used to reconfigure

---

33 In our three previous chapters we aimed to open up this discussion in a more interactive and provisional way. In light of the ever increasing stream of scientific data coming forward, it is crucial to present carefully formulated thoughts and fresh interpretations to explore the possibility of new horizons that may better reflect reality.

34 D. J. Linden, "The Religious Impulse," in: *The Accidental Mind: How Brain Evolution Has Given Us Love, Memory, Dreams, and God*, Cambridge: Belknap Press, 2007, presents an introductory summary of the neuropsychological research that supports such a conclusion.

and orient our thoughts. Once formed, these narrative worlds can be fixed in a written text where they function as wells of reflective energy that can be experienced over and over again. On closer examination, putting thoughts into meaningful patterns that create unique and imaginative worlds involves complex interactions between time, narrative, and history.

Deep inroads were carved into our understanding of these interactions with Ricoeur's publication of two key books: his three volume work, *Temps et récit* (*Time and Narrative*) and *La Mémoire, l'Histoire, l'Oubli* (*Memory, History, Forgetting*).[35] This section will draw on these works to reinforce the idea that time, narrative, and history function like a three-dimensional blueprint for constructing meaningful and coherent worlds. By examining this blueprint, the identity of the world represented in Genesis 2-3, whom it is referring to, and how it was meant to function should begin to materialize.[36]

Genesis 2-3, like much of biblical narrative, is a product of dynamic, pattern-building forces. The following description of this process is based on Ricoeur's analysis of narrative construction in general. It begins when selected thoughts, actions, and purposes converge at a particular point in time. This production stage, referred to as prefiguration, precedes the configuration of the text and sets the orientation and purpose of it. Configuration then becomes a matter of arranging and shaping this raw material into a coherent narrative whole with temporal properties. What emerges from this story configuration is a plot that can function in a couple of ways that apply to the interpretation of early Genesis. First, the plot can provide a dramatic vehicle for exploring and mediating any thoughts about God, humanity, and

---

35 Ricoeur, *Time and Narrative, vols. I-III*, and *Memory, History, Forgetting*, Chicago : University of Chicago Press, 2006.

36 See our three previous chapters for more on time, narrative, and history as it pertains to the science and theology discussion.

the world that are hard to reconcile or comprehend. Second, plots create a habitable dwelling place wherein the reader enters into a world of reflection. This world of reflection emerges out of a conceptual world that is context-dependent. Therefore, the narrative world will resonate with the concerns and realities of the time.[37] With these points in mind, biblical narrative can be envisioned as a time-sensitive literary construction that creates a conceptual space where thoughts about God's identity, human identity, and world identity can be formalized and entertained in provocative ways. Whatever concerns exist about how the narrative world fits with scientific-like descriptions fade into irrelevancy in this functional light.

What begins to take shape is the idea that the extravagant and imaginative images that form the tension filled plots of Genesis 2-3 function as a narrative seedbed for planting and exploring difficult ideas about God, humanity, and the world. The narrative world that emerges from this spiced-up theological cocktail not only resonates and coerces reflective thought, but it attempts to harmonize and interpret beginnings in light of the limited knowledge the ancient Hebrews had about God and the world in which they lived.

In order to understand the configuration of Genesis 2-3 that this chapter is proposing, it is worth re-emphasizing that the ancient Hebrews lived at a time when the details of the primordial past were virtually unknown and *unknowable*. There is no indication that they had detailed or paradigm-breaking knowledge about the natural world that would have set them apart from other cultures. This becomes evident when one considers how profoundly our present-day scientific understanding of origins collides with the literal interpretation of early Genesis. However, for the proposed narrative configuration offered below, disparity is to

---

37 See chapter 3.

be expected. What can be said with some degree of confidence is that the ancient Hebrew's understood Yahweh to be the creative and ruling authority over all things—past, present, and future.

As mentioned before, when we read this creation story we enter into a theo-poetic account of a *world beginning* freed from exacting certitude. A vision of the world is being offered that surpasses any depiction of the world based solely on the empirical side of the equation. Through the formula of a dramatic plot, the narrative lays down theological parameters that match and connect to the ancient Hebrew understanding of God's dramatic mission for Israel and the world. For instance, the drama in Eden exposes the identity of God, humanity, and the world that matches the Divine agenda already in progress. Whatever features of the physical world that do enter the story line more than likely serve as props to support this grand scheme.

Recall that in biblical times, primordial history was ungraspable in nature. This idea along with the preceding discussion provides support for the proposal that the interpretive option that best fits Genesis 2-3 is one akin to a *possible world* configuration. It is a configuration that enshrines the ancient Hebrew's theological reflections about the world of beginnings. The possible world perspective fits well with the idea that the narrative is a vision of time immemorial lodged in the ungraspable past. It is, therefore, an imaginative vision that had to be based off the real-time experiences and communications between God and Israel; communications that were primarily concerned with Israel's faithfulness and destiny. This means that the ancient narrative stands in a place where it is neither a decisive statement about the natural history of beginnings nor an unfounded re-description of reality.

The obvious question that erupts out of this discussion is how does one view the historicity of the story if a possible world view of Genesis 2-3 is adopted? It should be noted that in its present form, early Genesis probably represents a relatively recent redaction of various streams of thought and traditions in the Hebrew community.[38] This further supports the idea that there was a hard calculus going on in configuring the text. Nonetheless, the question still remains: what can be made of the historical tenor of the text?

Referring back to Ricoeur's work for assistance, he described three different types of historiography. Without going into a detailed analysis of his classification scheme and assuming that one of these types is applicable, the designation that would most closely fit Genesis 2-3 is the poetic one.[39] Briefly stated, a poetic theological historiography can be loaded with extravagant symbols and does not require a straight-telling of history.[40] In many respects, this designation with its poetic freedom complements the ideas that early Genesis is a proto-history and that uncertainties about beginnings abounded.

While this might be correct to some extent, the risk of extracting too much historical detail from the text remains. The way in which the Eden narrative flows into the history of Israel makes this tendency a likely course of action. But, when the poetic theological historiographical tone of the story is blended with the possible world configuration and the view that the biblical author is an interpreter himself, a hermeneutical shift occurs. This shift moves the hermeneutical focus away from literalistic tendencies and toward an interpretation that encompasses the exploratory character and purpose of the narrative. This hermeneutical redirection implies that historical precision could not have been the primary objective of the story.

---

38 Hyers, "Comparing Biblical and Scientific Maps of Origins," in: *Perspectives of an Evolving Creation*, K. B. Miller, ed., Grand Rapids: Eerdmans, 2003, 21-24.

39 See chapter 2.

40 Alter, *The Art of Biblical Narrative*, Long, *The Art of Biblical History*, T. Longman, "Storytellers and Poets in the Bible: Can Literary Artifice Be True?," in: *Inerrancy and Hermeneutic: A Tradition, A Challenge, A Debate*, H. Conn, ed., 137-149; Sternberg, *The Poetics of Biblical Narrative: Ideological Literature and the Drama of Reading*, all have illuminating insights on this matter.

By framing the historical element in this more hermeneutical way, it becomes feasible to view Genesis 2-3 with its possible world construct, as a *founding* narrative. That is, the text functioned as a sacred foundation for the Hebrew community, grounding their unfolding history in the fundamental beginning of all things. The God who was creating their nation was the same God who had created the world. This connection makes the narrative appear and function as proto-history. Thus, Genesis 2-3's founding function creates a theological backdrop from which the future can unfold under the auspices of Yahweh. Once the Eden narrative is elevated to this founding level, it becomes available for future theological reflections and linkages.

In summary, this brief examination of time, narrative, and history has attempted to show that the possible world interpretation of Genesis 2-3 is a viable hermeneutical option. This option promotes the idea that a story was created as a projection onto beginnings in order to fix paradigmatic founding ideas in the unfathomable depths of time immemorial. Thus, the dramatic plot that unfurls in the colorful world of Eden, full of symbolic extravagance, provides the highly animated vehicle needed to explore and achieve this purpose.

Separation: Identifying the *Who* of Beginnings

The concept of separation played an important role in the cognitive environment of the ancient Near East. In this setting, something was understood to come into existence once it had been separated out, named, and given a function.[41] Since the separation motif was a common ontological expression in ancient times, it is not surprising to find it used in the biblical text. For example, acts of separation in the week of creation (Gen. 1) have been well recognized. While this motif certainly exists in Genesis 2-3, it has

---

41 See chapter 2.

generally received less emphasis as a critical organizing principle in these chapters.

The contention of this chapter is that not only does this motif form a significant part of the narrative's design, but it further indicates that Genesis 2-3 is a well thought-out founding calculus. In this case, the calculus is framed with a possible world scenario that identifies the key players in a drama of beginnings. In other words, what forms with the aid of the separation motif is a medium of contrast where identities can be explored, expressed, and accounted for when there is a paucity of knowledge about beginnings. Therefore, God, evil, humanity, and the world take center stage.

Ricoeur took note of the presence and importance of this motif for the interpretation of the Eden narrative.[42] He pointed out that Genesis 2-3, which consists of two half narratives, exhibits a progression of separations. They begin with the creation of man (body and spirit) and culminate with the expulsion of the human pair from a sanctuary-like paradise. From this point on, life continues in an outside world of struggle and turmoil. There can be little doubt that the separation motif is prevalent in the narrative. This lends further credence to the idea that the author built the story using the conceptual tool kit common to his time. However, the pertinent question for this study is: how does the occurrence of the separation motif support the idea of a possible world interpretation of Genesis 2-3?

To see how this might be the case, take a closer look at the temptation scene through the dual lens of separation and possible worlds. It is clearly the most decisive moment in the story and is marked by the puzzling absence of God's presence.[43] Why did God leave a naked and naïve human pair alone to face the wiles of

---

42 Ricoeur and LaCocque, *Thinking Biblically*, 31-67. Narrative form is well suited to represent the multiplicity of God's creative acts and to feature an unfolding separation, which are then woven together into a revelatory whole.

43 The particular separation configuration of Divine and human, as well as Creator and creature, opens up the possibility for God to be absent in the story while the creature is present.

a persuasive, worldly-wise adversary? What chance did they have? The story generates a set of unanswerable *'what if'* questions, unless one shifts focus to a possible world interpretive perspective. Then, one of the main purposes of the story, and the temptation scene in particular, revolves around the artistic expression of identity. Thereby, the scenes in the Eden narrative reveal critical characteristics relating to God, humanity, evil, and the world from an ancient Hebrew perspective. For example, God is both the architect of all things and yet, through the separation strategy, God is partitioned off from those aspects of the world that seem contrary to His nature. With this in mind and with identity as one of the primary concerns of the narrative, it makes sense that the temptation scene would have God nowhere in sight when the poor decision is made by Adam and Eve. Through the dynamics of separation, God's identity remains unblemished by the actions of His creatures. In a sense, the scene represents a profound statement about how the Divine Architect must have a degree of distance from the profane things of the world, even though they are inexplicably already there.

Although there are many more examples of separation in the narrative and each one deserves a thorough treatment, space does not permit it here. Suffice it to say, that when the separation component of the Eden narrative is emphasized, at least two points about the function of the story become evident. First, it can be said that the separation motif allows the narrative to develop an image of the essential character, nature, and roles of the key participants in the beginning. By delineating these identities, Genesis 2-3 can fulfill its founding role. Second, use of the separation concept permits the formulation of pre-modern explanations that function to quarantine off some of life's more negative aspects from the good intentions of Divine creativity. In other words, the structure of separation creates a means of accounting for the unseemly things found in the world that leaves Divine integrity intact.

The Divine curses are a case in point. If one views the delivery of curses from the standpoint of separation, it becomes possible to interpret them as separating God's good plans for the world from the negative features of living life in the world. At the same time, God's overriding authority over everything in the world is upheld and intensified as the one who delivers the curses. Therefore, the curses are not simply outdated explanations; they are complex story elements that bring out the character of things as understood in ancient times. Conceptually speaking, one result of this re-visioning of the curses is that a stage is set that opens the gates into a forward-looking possible world of redemption and transformation that will progressively play out in the *actual* world.

Based on these comments, it seems reasonable to conclude that one of the primary functions of the text is to sharpen the image of God, humanity, evil, and the world and establish some of the primary relationships between them. It follows that whenever explanations for natural phenomena are given in the story, their over arching purpose is not to lay down data points about origins, but to help clarify the identity and function of the leading players in the act of beginnings. Therefore, the text does not represent a set of final explanations about how the natural world came to be, nor does it resolve all the sticky theological questions hovering around God's specific actions in the beginning. Consequently, a measure of mystery remains in the text.

In the final analysis, this discussion on the occurrence and function of separation in the Genesis 2-3 story contributes to the winnowing down of hermeneutical options. The present study proposes that the possible world view of Genesis 2-3 becomes a strong interpretive option when the story is understood as a composite of separation concepts, symbolic architecture, and founding narrative properties. It is an option that strikes an interpretive equilibrium between multiple hermeneutical factors.

Conclusion

In speaking of poetry and myth, Paul Ricoeur stated that, "They constitute a disclosure of unprecedented worlds, an opening on to other *possible* worlds which transcend the established limits of our *actual* world."[44] As this chapter has shown, Genesis 2-3 is armed with theo-poetic language and vivid symbolic/mythical architecture that is fitting for an ancient Near Eastern portrayal of beginnings where details are in short supply. Therefore, following the lead of Ricoeur, Genesis 2-3 can best be understood as a possible world depiction of the elusive primordial past. The possible world view leads to three major conclusions about the interpretation of the Eden narrative. First, it must be interpreted from the directional perspective that it is a *backward-facing* view into the unknown depths of the past. Second, the author himself is interpreting beginnings. And third, the author's interpretation is strongly connected to the ancient Hebrew's *understanding of their actual* world. This makes the narrative's construction dependent on the conceptual and literary conventions of the ancient Near East. The narrative, therefore, does not offer paradigm-breaking knowledge about natural history. Thus, Genesis 2-3 is a theo-poetic, symbol-laden story that transcends the normal operations of space and time in order to *explore* time immemorial.

This chapter depended heavily on the phenomenological concept of worlds to examine the Genesis 2-3 story. When this concept is applied to the interpretation of texts, the primary concern of hermeneutics becomes one in which the reader must deal "with the *worlds* which...authors and texts open up."[45] In the case of Genesis 2-3, the exotic depiction of life in the Garden of Eden creates a world where God and His creation are portrayed as having intimate contact in an *idealized sacred space*. It is in this *sanctu-*

---

44 M. J. Valdes, *A Ricoeur Reader: Reflection and Imagination*, Toronto: University of Toronto Press, 1991, 490.

45 Ibid. 490.

ary-like possible world where thoughts about God, His identity in contrast to others, and His interactions with the created order can be imagined, explored, and connected to the actual world. The presence of sanctuary/temple symbolism in the narrative corresponds with the viewpoint that Genesis 2-3 is an exploratory account connected to the unique religious identity of the ancient Hebrews. Thus, Genesis 2-3 with its possible world construct *becomes* a founding narrative.

Science continues to supply overwhelming details about the evolutionary nature of the material world. The interpretive option presented in this study moves Genesis 2-3 away from explanatory excesses that are irrelevant to its founding purposes. It follows that Genesis 2-3 gives minimal information about how the world began.[46] Therefore, the tendency to pit Genesis 2-3 as an alternate view of the natural world over and against an evolutionary view totally misses the mark.[47]

There are many moving parts in this possible world/founding narrative schema that give rise to a host of questions. For example, how far can this approach extend? Does it incorporate the proto-history of the first eleven chapters of Genesis? Even more perplexing, what is one to make of Paul's usage of Adam? Does Paul's interpretation of Adam negate the possible world interpretation?[48] These questions underscore the complexity of coming to terms with Genesis 2-3.

---

46 Gen. 2-3 may be a marginal text. For example, "within the Hebrew Bible itself the story of Adam and Eve is nowhere cited as the explanation for sin and evil in the world." J. Barr, *The Garden of Eden and the Hope of Immortality*, Minneapolis: Fortress Press, 1993, 6. Adam is in *suspended animation* for the most part until Paul picks up the story and *reinterprets it in* "Hellenistic times," Barr, 18. Ricoeur, *Symbolism of Evil*, 235-243, draws attention to matters like this and notes that "it is false that the 'Adamic' myth is the keystone of the Judeo-Christian edifice; it is only a flying buttress, articulated upon the ogival crossing of the Jewish penitential spirit."

47 P. Enns, *The Evolution of Adam: What the Bible Does and Doesn't Say about Human Origins*, Grand Rapids: Brazos Press, 2012, reinforces this point.

48 Paul's use of Adam would appear to negate the possible world option, but this need not be the case. If Gen. 2-3 is the kind of founding narrative discussed in this chapter, then Paul may simply be connecting into it as an apologetic resource for emphasizing the identity of Jesus—just like the possible world is emphasizing the identity of the God (Yahweh) who the ancient Hebrews have actually encountered. The fact that Adam may be figurative and representative in the possible world story and used for comparative purposes does not negate the historical figure of Christ. It emphasizes the founding narrative status of Gen. 2-3.

In conclusion, the *possible world/founding narrative paradigm* offers a general hermeneutical strategy for approaching Genesis 2-3. It offers a research direction that encourages engagement with the evolutionary picture of the natural world. The adoption of this approach allows new interpretive and integrative possibilities to emerge that deepen our understanding of God, the text, ourselves, and the world.

BIBLIOGRAPHY

Alioto, A. *A History of Western Science*. Englewood Cliffs: Prentice Hall. 1993.

Alcock, J. *The Triumph of Sociobiology*. Oxford: Oxford University Press. 2001.

Alter, R. *The Art of Biblical Narrative*. New York: Basic Books. 1981.

Anderson, B. W. *Creation versus Chaos*. Philadelphia: Fortress. 1987.

Aristotle. *Physics*. D. Bostock ed., Trans. R. Waterfield. New York: Oxford University Press. 2008.
_____. *Poetics*, Dover: Thrift Editions, 1997.

Augustine. *St. Augustine on Genesis: On the Literal interpretation of Genesis: An Unfinished Book*. Trans. R. J. Teske. Catholic University Press of America: Wash. D.C. 1991.
_____. *Confessions*. Trans. Introduction and Notes, H. Chadwick. Oxford: Oxford University Press. 1991.

Atkins, P. "The Limitless Power of Science," in: J. Cornwell, ed., *Nature's Imagination: The Frontiers of Scientific Vision*, Oxford: Oxford Univ. Press, 1995, 122-132.

Barbour, I. G. *When Science Meets Religion*. New York: HarperCollins. 2000.
_____. *Religion in an Age of Science*. San Francisco: HarperCollins. 1990.

Barr, J. *The Garden of Eden and the Hope of Immortality.* Minneapolis: Fortress Press. 1993.

Bartholomew, C. G. and R. P. O'Dowd. *Old Testament Wisdom Literature: A Theological Introduction.* Downers Grove: IVP. 2011.

Baudrillard, J. *The Perfect Crime.* Trans. C. Turner. London: Verso. 1996.

Beale, G. K. "Eden, the Temple, and the Church's Mission in New Creation," *Evangelical Theological Society 48/1* (2005), 5-31.
_____. *The Temple and the Church's Mission: A Biblical Theology of the Dwelling Place of God.* Downers Grove: IVP. 2004.

Beauchamp, P. *Création et separation.* Paris: Desclée. 1969.
_____. "Le serpent herméneute," in: *L'Un et L'Autre Testament, vol. 2,* Paris: Seuil 1990, 137-158.

Blocher, H. "Biblical Reference and Historical Reference," *Scottish Bulletin of Evangelical Theology 3* (1989), 102-122.
_____. *In the Beginning: The Opening Chapters of Genesis.* Downers Grove: Intervarsity Press. 1984.

Brooke, J. H. *Science and Religion: Some Historical Perspectives.* Cambridge: Cambridge Univ. Press. 1991.

Bube, R. H. *Putting It All Together: Seven Patterns for Relating Science and the Christian Faith.* Lanham: Univ. Press of America. 1995.

Caird, G. B. *The Language and Imagery of the Bible.* Philadelphia: Westminster. 1980.

Carr, D. "Ricoeur on Narrative," in: D. Wood, ed., *On Paul Ricoeur: Narrative and Interpretation,* London: Routledge, 1991, 160-187.

Clayton, P. D. *God and Contemporary Science.* Edinburgh: Edinburgh University Press. 1997.

Coleridge, S. T. *The Complete Poems.* William Keach, ed., London & New York: Penguin Books, 1997.

Collins, F. S. *The Language of God: A Scientist Presents Evidence for Belief.* New York: Free Press. 2006.

Comstock, G. L. "Truth or Meaning: Ricoeur versus Frei on Biblical Narrative," *Journal of Religion 66* (1986), 117-140.
_____. "Two Types of Narrative Theology," *Journal of the American Academy of Religion 55/4* (1987), 687-717.

Crick, F. *The Astonishing Hypothesis: The Scientific Search for the Soul.* New York: Scribner. 1994.

Davies, P. R. and J. Rogerson. *The Old Testament World.* Englewood Cliffs: Prentice Hall. 1989.

Dawkins, R. *The Blind Watchmaker: Why the evidence of evolution reveals a universe without design.* New York: W.W. Norton. 1987.
_____. *The God Delusion.* Boston: Houghton Mifflin. 2006.

Debus, A. G. *Man and Nature in the Renaissance.* Cambridge: Cambridge University Press. 1978.

Dembski, W. *Intelligent Design: The Bridge Between Science & Theology.* Downers Grove: Intervarsity Press. 1999.

Dennett, D. *Breaking The Spell: Religion as a Natural Phenomenon.* New York: Viking. 2006.
_____. *Darwin's Dangerous Idea: Evolution and the Meanings of Life.* New York: Simon & Schuster. 1995.
_____. *Freedom Evolves.* New York: Viking. 2003.

Doukhan, J. B. *The Genesis Creation Story: Its Literary Structure.* Berrien Springs: Andrews University Press. 1978.

Duce, P. "Complementarity in Perspective," *Perspectives on Science and Christian Faith, 8* (1996), 145-155.
_____. *Reading the mind of God: Interpretation in Science and Theology.* Leicester: Apollos. 1998.

Eliot, T. S. *The Four Quartets,* London: Faber & Faber, 1959.

Emmrich, M. "The Temptation Narrative of Genesis 3: 1-6: A Prelude to the Pentateuch and the History of Israel," *Evangelical Quarterly 73* 1 (2001), 3-20.

Enns, P. *The Evolution of Adam: What the Bible Does and Doesn't Say about Human Origins.* Grand Rapids: Brazos Press. 2012.

Feyerabend, P. *Against Method.* London: Verso. 1975.

Frei, H. W. *The Eclipse of Biblical Narrative: A Study in Eighteenth and Nineteenth Century Hermeneutics.* New Haven: Yale University Press. 1974.
_____. "The 'Literal Reading' of Biblical Narrative in the Christian Tradition: Does it Stretch or Will it Break?" in: F. McConnell, ed., *The Bible and the Narrative Tradition,* Oxford: Oxford University Press, 1986, 36-77.

Gould, S. J. *Ever Since Darwin: Reflections in Natural History,* New York: W. W. Norton. 1977.

Gregersen, N. H. "Theology in a Neo-Darwinian World," *Studia Theologica 48* (1994), 125-149.

Halpern, B. *The First Historians: The Hebrew Bible and History.* University Park: Pennsylvania State University Press. 1996.

Haught, J. F. *Making Sense of Evolution: Darwin, God, and the Drama of Life.* Louisville: John Knox Press. 2010.

Hawking, S. *A Brief History of Time: From the Big Bang to Black Holes.* London: Bantam Press. 1988.

Hooke, S. H. ed., *Myth, Ritual, and Kingship.* Oxford: Clarendon. 1958.

Hopkins, G. M. *Poems,* London: Humphery Milford, 1918.

Hyers, C. *Meaning of Creation: Genesis and Modern Science.* Atlanta: John Knox Press. 1984.
_____. "Comparing Biblical and Scientific Maps of Origins," in: K. B. Miller, ed., *Perspectives of an Evolving Creation,* Grand Rapids: Eerdmans, 2003, 21-24.

Ihde, D. *Hermeneutic Phenomenology.* Evanston: Northwestern University Press. 1971.

Jackelén, A. "Science and Religion: Getting Ready for the Future," *Zygon: Journal of Religion and Science 38* (June 2003), 209-228.

Jeeves, M. A. and R. J. Berry. *Science, Life, and Christian Belief: A Survey of Contemporary Issues.* Grand Rapids: Baker Books. 1998.

Jenkins, K. *Re-Thinking History.* London: Routledge. 1991.
_____. ed., *The Postmodern History Reader.* London: Routledge. 1997.

Johnson, P. *Reason in the Balance: The Case Against NATURALISM in Science, Law & Education.* Downers Grove: Intervarsity Press. 1995.

Kuhn, T. S. *The Structure of Scientific Revolutions.* Second Edition, Chicago: The Univ. of Chicago Press. 1970.

Laughery, G. J. "Ricoeur on History, Fiction and Biblical Hermeneutics," in: C. Bartholomew, C. S. Evans, M. Healy, M. Rae, eds., *"Behind" the Text: History and Biblical Interpretation*. Grand Rapids/ Carlisle: Zondervan/ Paternoster, 2003, 339-362.
_____. *Living Hermeneutics in Motion: An Analysis and Evaluation of Paul Ricoeur's Contribution to Biblical Hermeneutics*. Lanham: Univ. Press of America. 2002. Revised edition *Living Hermeneutics*, forthcoming 2015.
_____. "Language at the Frontiers of Language," in: Craig Bartholomew, Colin Greene, Karl Möller, eds., *After Pentecost: Language and Biblical Interpretation*, Carlisle: Paternoster, 2001, 171-194.

Lewis, C. S. "Myth Became Fact," in: W. Hooper, ed., *God in the Dock*, Grand Rapids: Eerdmans, 1990, 63-67.
_____. "On Stories," in: Walter Hooper, ed., *Of This and Other Worlds*, London: Collins, 1982, 25-45.

Linden, D. J. *The Accidental Mind: How Brain Evolution Has Given Us Love, Memory, Dreams, and God.* Cambridge: Belknap Press. 2007.

Livingstone, D. *Darwin's Forgotten Defenders: The Encounter Between Evangelical Theology and Evolutionary Thought.* Vancouver: Regent College Publishing. 1984.

Long, V. P. *The Art of Biblical History.* Grand Rapids: Zondervan. 1994.

Longman, T. "Storytellers and Poets in the Bible: Can Literary Artifice Be True?" in: H. Conn, ed., *Inerrancy and Hermeneutic: A Tradition, A Challenge, A Debate,* Grand Rapids: Baker, 1988, 137-149.

Lucas, E. *Interpreting Genesis in the 21st Century*, Faraday Paper No 11. Cambridge: The Faraday Institute for Science and Religion. 2007.

_____. "Science and the Bible: Are They Incompatible?" *Science and Christian Belief XVII* (2005), 137-154.

Lyotard, J-F. *The Postmodern Condition: A Report on Knowledge.* Trans. Geoff Bennington and Brian Massumi, Minneapolis: Univ. of Minnesota Press. 1984.

Mackay, D. M. *The Clockwork Image: A Christian Perspective on Science.* Downers Grove: Intervarsity Press. 1974.

Mann, T. *Der Zauberberg.* Roman. Fischer Taschenbuch Verlag: Frankfurt. 1924.
_____. *The Magic Mountain.* Trans. J. E. Woods. Vintage: New York. 1996.

Marguerat, D. *La première histoire du christianisme.* Paris: Cerf. 1999.
_____. *The First Christian Historian.* Trans. G. J. Laughery, K. McKinney, R. Bauckham. Cambridge: Cambridge University Press, 2002.

Marion, J-L. *Being Given: Toward A Phenomenology of Givenness.* Trans. J. L. Kosky. Stanford: Stanford University Press. 2002.
_____. *Etant donné: Essai d'une phénoménologie de la donation.* Paris: Presses Universitaires de France. 1997.

Marsden, G. *Fundamentalism and American Culture: The Shaping of Twentieth-Century Evangelicalism: 1870-1925.* Oxford: Oxford Univ. Press. 1980.

Miller, K. B. ed., *Perspectives on an Evolving Creation,* Grand Rapids: Eerdmans. 2003.

Miller, K. R. *Finding Darwin's God: A Scientist's Search for Common Ground Between God and Evolution.* New York: HarperCollins. 1999.

Moore, J. A. *Science as a Way of Knowing: The Foundations of Modern Biology*. Cambridge, MA: Harvard Univ. Press. 1993.

Morrow, J. "Creation as Temple-Building and Work as Liturgy in Genesis 1-3," *Journal of the Orthodox Center for the Advancement of Biblical Studies* (2009), 1-13.

Munslow, A. *Deconstructing History*. London: Routledge. 1997.

Nielsen, K. "Searching for an Emancipatory Perspective: Wide Reflective Equilibrium and the Hermeneutical Circle," in: E. Simpson, ed., *Anti-Foundationalism and Practical Reasoning*, Edmonton, AB: Academic Press, 1987, 143-163.

Noll, M. A. *The Scandal of the Evangelical Mind*. Grand Rapids: Eerdmans. 1994.

Polanyi, M. *Personal Knowledge: Towards a Post-Critical Philosophy*. Chicago: The Univ. of Chicago Press. 1958.

Polkinghorne, J. *Reason and Reality: The Relationship between Science & Theology*. Philadelphia: Trinity Press International. 1991.
_____. *Belief in God in an Age of Science*. New Haven: Yale Univ. Press. 1998.
_____. *Faith, Science & Understanding*. New Haven: Yale Univ. Press. 2000.

Preminger, A. ed., *The Princeton Encyclopedia of Poetry and Poetics*. London: Macmillan. 1975.

Ramm, B. *The Christian View of Science and Scripture*. Grand Rapids: Eerdmans. 1954.

Ricoeur, P. *Essays on Biblical Interpretaion*. L. S. Mudge, ed., Philadelphia: Fortress, 1980.
_____. *Figuring the Sacred: Religion, Narrative, and Imagination*. M. I. Wallace, ed., Trans. D. Pellauer. Minneapolis: Fortress. 1995.
_____. *From Text to Action, Essays in Hermeneutics, II*. Trans. Kathleen Blamey and John B. Thompson, Evanston: Northwestern Univ. Press. 1991.
_____. *History and Truth*. Bloomington: Northwestern University Press. 1955.
_____. *Interpretation Theory: Discourse and the Surplus of Meaning*. Fort Worth: Texas Christian University Press. 1976.
_____. *La bible en philosophie*. Paris: Cerf. 1993.
_____. "My Relation to the History of Philosophy," *The Iliff Review 35* (1978), 5-12.
_____."Philosophies critiques de l'histoire: Recherche, explication, écriture," in: G. Fløistad, ed., *Philosophical problems today, vol 1*, Dordrecht : Kluwer, 1994, 139-201.
_____. *Philosophie de la volonté. Finitude et culpabilité II, La symbolique du mal*. Paris: Aubier. 1960.
_____. "Science and Ideology," in: J.B. Thompson, Trans. and ed., *Hermeneutics and the Human Sciences*, Cambridge: Cambridge University Press, 1981, 222-246.
_____."Sur l'exégèse de Genèse 1,1-2,4a," in: Leon Dufour, ed., *Exégèse et herméneutique*, Paris : Seuil, 1971, 57-97.
_____. *Temps et récit*. 3 vols. Paris: Seuil. 1983-1985.
_____. *Time and Narrative*. 3 vols. Trans. K. McLaughlin and D. Pellauer, vols. 1-2; K. Blamey and D. Pellauer, vol. 3. Chicago: University of Chicago Press. 1984-1987.
_____. *The Conflict of Interpretations, Essays in Hermeneutics*, D. Ihde, ed., Evanston: Northwestern University Press. 1974.
_____. *The Symbolism of Evil*, Trans. E. Buchanan, New York: Harper & Row. 1967.

Ricoeur, P., J. M. Brohm and M. Uhl. "Arts, Language and Hermeneutic Aesthetics," An interview by J.-M. Brohm and M. Uhl, September 1996.

Ricoeur, P. and J-P. Changeux. *Ce qui nous fait penser? La nature et la règle.* Paris: Odile Jacob. 2000.
_____. *What Makes us Think? A Neuroscientist and A Philosopher Argue About Ethics, Human Nature and the Brain.* Trans. M. B. DeBevoise. Princeton: Princeton University Press. 2002.

Ricoeur, P. and A. LaCocque. *Penser la bible.* Paris: Seuil. 1998.
_____. *Thinking Biblically.* Trans. D. Pellauer. Chicago: University of Chicago Press, 1998.

Rouse, J. *Engaging Science: How to Understand Its Practices Philosophically.* thaca: Cornell Univ. Press. 1996.

Ruse, M. and Edward O. Wilson. "The Approach of Sociobiology: The Evolution of Ethics," in: James E. Huchingson, ed., *Religion and the Natural Sciences: The Range of Engagement*, Orlando: Harcourt Brace, 1993, 308-312.

Sagan, C. *The Demon-Haunted World: Science as a Candle in the Dark.* New York: Ballantine Books. 1996.

Sailhamer, J. H. *An Introduction to Old Testament Theology: A Canonical Approach.* Grand Rapids: Zondervan. 1995.
_____. *The Pentateuch as Narrative.* Grand Rapids: Zondervan. 1992.

Saunders, N. *Divine Action and Modern Science.* Cambridge: Cambridge Univ. Press. 2002.

Scharlemann, R. P. "The Textuality of Texts," in: D. E. Klemm and W. Schweiker, eds., *Meaning in Texts and Actions: Questioning Paul Ricoeur*, Charlottesville: University Press of Virginia, 1993, 13-25.

Schrag, Calvin O. *The Self After Postmodernity.* New Haven: Yale Univ. Press. 1997.
_____. *The Resources of Rationality.* Bloomington: ndiana Univ. Press. 1992.

Schwarz, Hans. *Creation.* Grand Rapids: Eerdmans. 2002.

Segal, R. A. ed., *Philosophy, Religious Studies, and Myth.* New York: Garland. 1996.

Simkins, R. A. *Creator & Creation.* Peabody: Hendrickson. 1994.

Smith, J. K. A. *The Fall of Interpretation: Philosophical Foundations for a Creational Hermeneutic.* Downers Grove: IVP. 2000.

Speiser, E. A. "The Rivers of Paradise," in: J. J. Finkelstein and M. Greenberg, eds., *Oriental and Biblical Studies: Collected Writings of E. A. Speiser*, Philadelphia: University of Pennsylvania Press, 1967, 23-34.

Sternberg, M. *The Poetics of Biblical Narrative: Ideological Literature and the Drama of Reading.* Bloomington: Indiana University Press. 1985.

Stiver, D. R. *Theology After Ricoeur: New Directions in Hermeneutical Theology.* Louisville: Westminster John Knox. 2001.

Stordalen, T. *Echoes of Eden: Genesis 2-3 and the Symbolism of the Eden Garden in Biblical Hebrew Literature.* Leuven: Peeters. 2000.

Tarkovsky, A. *Sculpting in Time.* Trans. K. Hunter-Blair. Austin: University of Texas Press. 1986.

Tolkien, J. R. R. "On Fairy Stories," in: *The Tolkien Reader*, New York: Ballantine, 1966, 33-99.

Valdes, M. J. *A Ricoeur Reader: Reflection and Imagination.* Toronto: University of Toronto Press. 1991.

Vanhoozer, K. J. "What is Everyday Theology?' in: Vanhoozer, C. A. Anderson, M. J. Sleasman, eds., *Everyday Theology: How to Read Cultural Texts and Interpret Trends,* Grand Rapids: Baker, 2007, 15-60.
_____. "On the Very Idea of a Theological System: An Essay in Triangulating Scripture, Church and World," in: A.T. B. McGowan, ed., *Always Reforming: Explorations in Systematic Theology,* Downers Grove: IVP, 2006, 125-182.
_____. "Pilgrim's Digress: Christian Thinking on and about the Post/Modern Way," in: M. B. Penner, ed., *Christianity and the Postmodern Turn,* Grand Rapids: Brazos, 2005, 71-103.
_____. *Remythologizing Theology: Divine Action, Passion, and Authorship.* Cambridge: Cambridge University Press. 2010.
_____. *The Drama of Doctrine, A Canonical Linguistic Approach to Christian Theology.* Louisville: Westminster John Knox. 2005.

Van Huyssteen, J. Wentzel. *Alone in the World? Human Uniqueness in Science and Theology.* Grand Rapids: Eerdmans. 2006.
_____. *The Shaping of Rationality: Toward Interdisciplinarity in Theology and Science.* Grand Rapids: Eerdmans. 1999.
_____. *Duet or Duel? Theology and Science in a Postmodern World.* Harrisburg: Trinity Press International. 1998.

Van Till, H. J. "The Scientific Investigation of Cosmic History," in: Howard. J. Van Till, Robert E. Snow, John H. Stek, and Davis A. Young, *Portraits of Creation: Biblical and Scientific Perspectives on the World's Formation,* Grand Rapids: Eerdmans, 1990, 82-125.
_____. *The Fourth Day.* Grand Rapids: Eerdmans. 1986.

Vidal, N., J. Rage, A. Couloux, and S. B. Hedges, 'Snakes (Serpentes),' in: S. B Hedges and S. Kumar, eds., *The Timetree of Life.* Oxford: Oxford University Press, 2009, 390-397.

Walton, J. H. *Ancient Israelite Literature in its Cultural Context: A Survey of Parallels between Biblical and Ancient Near Eastern Texts.* Grand Rapids: Zondervan. 1990.
_____. *Ancient Near Eastern Thought and the Old Testament: Introducing the Conceptual World of the Old Testament.* Grand Rapids: Baker Academic. 2006.

Watts, F. "Science and Theology as Complementary Perspectives," in: N. H. Gregersen and J. W. van Huyssteen, eds., *Rethinking Theology and Science; Six Models for the Current Dialogue,* Grand Rapids: Eerdmans, 1998, 125-149.

Wenham, G. J. "Sanctuary Symbolism in the Garden of Eden Story," in: R. S. Hess and D. T. Tsumura, eds., *I Studied Inscriptions from Before the Flood: Ancient Near Eastern, Literary, and Linguistic Approaches to Genesis 1-11,* Winona Lake: Eisenbrauns, 1994, 399-404.

Westermann, C. *Creation* trans. J. J. Scullion, Philadelphia: Fortress. 1974.

Westphal, M. *Suspicion & Faith: The Religious uses of Modern Atheism.* Grand Rapids: Eerdmans. 1993.

Whitcomb, J. C. Jr. and H. M. Morris. *The Genesis Flood: The Biblical Record and Its Scientific Implications.* Philadelphia: Presbyterian and Reformed. 1961.

Wilson, E. O. *Sociobiology: the New Synthesis.* Cambridge: Harvard Univ. Press. 1975.
_____. *On Human Nature.* Cambridge, MA: Harvard Univ. Press. 1978.
_____. *Consilience.* New York: Knopf. 1998.

Wordsworth, W.
Ecclesiastical Sketches. 1822.

Wright, N. T.
The New Testament and the People of God. London: SPCK. 1992.

Young, D. A. 1990. "The Discovery of Terrestrial History," in: Howard. J. Van Till, Robert E. Snow, John H. Stek, and Davis A. Young, *Portraits of Creation: Biblical and Scientific Perspectives on the World's Formation,* Grand Rapids: Eerdmans, 1990, 26-81.

Zagorin, P. "History, the Referent, and Narrative Reflections on Postmodernism Now," *History and Theory 38* (1999), 1-24.

INDEX

Destinée Media

Destinée Media publishes both fiction and non-fiction, and aims to provide culturally engaging publications that bring a fresh perspective to spirituality and culture.

At Destinée Media we seek to operate by faith in God within a Biblical/Christian worldview. We hope to inspire 'culture making' by promoting ideas that will contribute to Christ being understood as Lord of the whole of life, which is to be marked by redemption and renewal. We are committed to reflecting carefully on vital matters for the church, academy, and society, while aiming to keep a personal and intimate dimension of the Christian life in view.

Destinée Media is interested in people and shares in several key aspects of the L'Abri ethos, (www.labri.org) including being innovative, living truth in love, and supporting the arts.

We thank you for your interest in our materials and hope that you find them both relevant and challenging. Please share your thoughts with us:

www.destineemedia.com

destinēe

CPSIA information can be obtained at www.ICGtesting.com
Printed in the USA
LVOW07s1144250215

428309LV00005B/380/P

9 781938 367199